OAHU

HOW TO USE THIS GUIDEBOOK

This guidebook is divided into four sections: *An Introduction to Oahu, The History of Oahu,* and *Oahu.*

The first two sections comprise essays, designed to provide you with facts on the area.

In the next two sections we explore Oahu, with a detailed, geographical breakdown of the area. Each section contains descriptions of the various places and points of interest, followed by a subsection entitled *Practical Information.* The *Practical Information* is designed to provide you with a ready reference to accommodations, restaurants, tours, places of interest, recreation areas, transportation, etc., with addresses and phone numbers.

A quick and easy way into this book is the *Index* at the end.

California Series

The Complete Gold Country Guidebook
The Complete Lake Tahoe Guidebook
The Complete Monterey Peninsula Guidebook
The Complete San Diego Guidebook
The Complete Wine Country Guidebook
Vacation Towns of California

Hawaii Series

The Complete Kauai Guidebook
The Complete Maui Guidebook
The Complete Oahu Guidebook
The Complete Big Island of Hawaii Guidebook

Outdoor Series

California Camper's Handbook
California State Parks Handbook

Adventure Series

An Adventurer's Guide to Humboldt County
An Adventurer's Guide to Mendocino County

Indian Chief Travel Guides are available from your local bookstore or Indian Chief Publishing House, P.O. Box 1814, Davis, California 95617.

Visit us at www.indianchief.net

The Complete
OAHU
Guidebook

Published by Indian Chief Publishing House
Davis, California

Text and Research: **David J. Russ**
Editor: **B. Sangwan**
Cover Art and Maps: **B.Sangwan**

Copyright © 2002 Indian Chief Publishing House

All rights reserved. No maps, illustrations, photographs, cover art, text, or other part of this book may be reproduced, in any form whatsoever, without written permission of the Publisher. For inquiries, address Indian Chief Publishing House, P.O. Box 1814, Davis, CA 95617. Inquiries via email may be sent to *mail@indianchief.net*.

ISBN 0-916841-68-5

Printed in the U.S.A.

CONTENTS

Map of Hawaiian Islands 6-7

Map of Oahu 8-9

AN INTRODUCTION TO OAHU — "The Aloha Island" 11

THE HISTORY OF OAHU 13

OAHU — "The Gathering Place" 18
Map of Oahu 20-21
Map of Downtown Honolulu 24-25
Map of Honolulu 30-31
Map of Waikiki 37
Map of East Honolulu 44
Map of North Shore 51
Map of Windward Coast 56
Map of Waianae Coast 63

Practical Information 67

HAWAIIAN GLOSSARY 113

INDEX 124

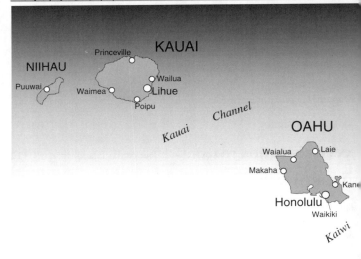

PACIFIC

OCEAN

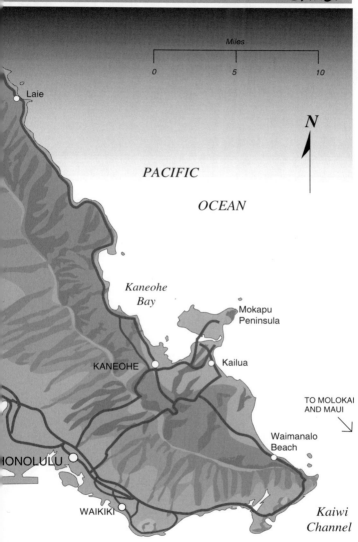

AN INTRODUCTION TO OAHU

"The Aloha Island"

Oahu is Hawaii's "Aloha Island." It is the most populous—and most popular—of the Hawaiian islands, with a population of around 850,000, and drawing more visitors than any other island in Hawaii. It also has in it the city of Honolulu, the state capital and largest metropolis in Hawaii, historic Pearl Harbor, and Waikiki, one of the most famous beach resorts in the world.

Oahu comprises approximately 608 square miles—the third largest of the Hawaiian islands—situated to the northwest of Molokai and Maui, 25 and 75 miles, respectively, with the island of Kauai to its northwest, some 95 miles distant. The island itself lies largely between two lush mountain ranges, Waianae and Ko'olau, with Honolulu lying to the south of the Ko'olau mountains, at the southeastern end of the island.

Nearly 5.5 million people visit Oahu each year, with many of them traveling only to Oahu, and some venturing further to the other islands. There are approximately 40,000 hotel rooms and condominium accommodations, more than 750 restaurants, and a wealth of recreational facilities—for swimming, snorkeling, scuba diving, surfing, windsurfing, sailing, boating, beachcombing, whale watching (in

Introduction

season), fishing, hiking, camping, horseback riding, tennis, golf, and more. Oahu also enjoys a delightful, temperate yet supremely varied climate, with temperatures ranging from 65° in the winter months to 85° or so in summer.

Indeed, Oahu is Hawaii's ultimate destination resort—the "Aloha Island!"

THE HISTORY OF OAHU

Oahu began forming nearly 6 million years ago—the result of a series of eruptions on the ocean floor that created two adjacent, shielded volcanoes, which, with the accumulation of molten lava over a period of time, finally emerged as Mount Ka'ala—at the head of the Waianae Range—and Konahuanui—the peak of the Ko'olau Range—some 4,020 feet and 3,150 feet above sea level, respectively, with a low, central isthmus—the Leilehua Plateau—between them, joining the two land masses. Then, approximately a million years ago, the two volcanoes became extinct, and in the following years, rivers, streams, ocean waves and the wind sculpted and shaped the island, with its valleys, canyons, cliffs and mountains; while a series of smaller, hydromagmatic explosions, some 150,000 years ago, formed the island's landmark volcanic cones—Diamond Head, Koko Head and Punchbowl.

An ancient Hawaiian myth, however, endures that Oahu and the other Hawaiian islands are the offspring of Papa, the earth deity, and Wakea, the divine embodiment of the sky, who arrived in this part of the Pacific from Tahiti. Papa and Wakea first conceived Hawaii, the big island, followed by Maui. Wakea then conceived with Kaulawahine—another deity—the island of Lanai, and with Hina, the island of Molokai. Papa, for her part, thoroughly infuriated, then conceived with Lua—a male deity—the island of Oahu. And finally, Papa and Wakea reconciled and together conceived Kauai and the nearby island of Ni'ihau.

In any case, Oahu's earliest inhabitants were the Marquesans, a Polynesian people who journeyed to Oahu from the Marquesas and Society islands between 500 A.D. and 750 A.D., followed some years

History

later, around 1000 A.D., by the Tahitians. The Marquesans, who journeyed to Hawaii in large outrigger canoes, navigating by the stars as they traveled across several miles of open ocean, introduced to Oahu and the other Hawaiian islands the first domestic animals, plants and fruit; and the Tahitians, for their part, brought with them their religion, their gods and goddesses, notable among them—Kane, the god of all living creatures; Ku, god of war; Pele, goddess of fire; Kaneloa, the god of the land of the departed spirits; and Lono, god of harvest and peace. The Tahitians also introduced to the islands the *kapu* system, a strict social order that affected all aspects of life, and became the core of ancient Hawaiian culture.

The first white man to sight Oahu was Captain James Cook, a British explorer in search of a northwest passage from the Pacific Ocean to the Atlantic Ocean. He first sighted Oahu on January 18, 1778, during his second expedition to the Pacific and the Hawaiian islands, but did not land on the island. In the following years, others followed, including Nathaniel Portlock and George Dixon—who had served under Cook—Captain George Vancouver, another British explorer, who dropped anchor off Waikiki in March, 1792, and William Brown, an English merchant sea captain, who first discovered Honolulu's harbor in 1793. These early Europeans, however, also brought with them to Oahu and the other Hawaiian islands the white man's disease. The Hawaiians, of course, had little or no resistance to Western diseases, and over a period of some 100 years following Cook's first contact with the islands, nearly 80% of the indigenous Hawaiian population had been wiped out.

The mid and late 1700s also ushered in Hawaii's era of monarchy. Kamehameha I—or Kamehameha the Great—was born in the late 1750s, and by 1791 he had gained control of the island of Hawaii, followed, in 1794, by the conquests of the nearby islands of Maui, Molokai and Lanai. The following year, in 1795, in his bid to unify all the Hawaiian islands under his rule, he also invaded and conquered Oahu, landing 16,000 warriors on the beach at Waikiki and driving the defenders of Oahu over the steep cliffs above Nu'uanu Valley, to their deaths. Finally, in 1810, Kamehameha extended his dominion, through diplomacy, to include Kauai, and subsequently established his capital in Lahaina, Maui, which, however, a few years later, in 1843, was shifted to Honolulu, on the island of Oahu.

In 1820, the first missionaries arrived in Oahu. Among the earliest and most notable, of course, was Hiram Bingham, who established that same year, on April 25, the first Christian church on the island, the Kawaiahao Church, which was then built some years later, in 1842, and quickly became Hawaii's most important church—the church of Hawaiian royalty, where kings and queens worshipped, and were coronated, married, and given their last rites as well. Other notable early-day missionaries on Oahu included Gerrit Judd, a contemporary of Bingham, and Elisha Loomis, who also established one of Hawaii's first printing presses, in Honolulu, to print English-Hawaiian translations of the Bible.

The mid-1800s witnessed the birth of Hawaii's sugar industry. Large sugarcane plantations were developed throughout the islands,

History   15

mostly by descendants of the early missionaries. On Oahu, in fact, some of Hawaii's largest sugar companies were established—among them Castle & Cooke, C. Brewer, American Factor and Theo H. Davies —which became charter members of Hawaii's Big Five—the islands' five largest corporations that produced and marketed nearly 96% of the islands' sugar, and controlled Hawaii's economy and politics for more than half a century. Hawaii now produces approximately 1 million tons of sugar annually, with only 16% coming from Oahu, largely from the 26,000 acres of sugarcane fields in Central Oahu's Leilehua Plateau.

The late 1800s and early 1900s also brought to the Hawaiian islands waves of immigrants—mostly Chinese, Japanese, Filipino, Portuguese and other Europeans—drawn to Hawaii's growing sugar and pineapple industries. The numbers of these new immigrants, of course, over time, turned Hawaii's indigenous population into a minority. On Oahu, in fact, pure-blooded, native Hawaiians now comprise only 15% of the population.

The late 19th century was also a period of transformation for the Hawaiian monarchy. In 1872, following the death of Kamehameha V, the last of the kings of the Kamehameha dynasty, the practise of electing a king was established, and in 1873, William Lunalilo became Hawaii's first king to be elected to the throne. Lunalilo, however, died the following year, in 1874, and was succeeded by David Kalakaua, who ruled until his death in January, 1891. Kalakaua, famous as the "Merrie Monarch," revived, during his reign, the Hawaiian culture, including missionary-banned Hawaiian music and the ancient dance of storytelling, the *hula*. He also composed Hawaii's national anthem, *"Hawaii Ponoi"*—or "Hawaii's Own"—and built in 1882, at a cost of $350,000, the glorious Iolani Palace, which remains today the nation's only royal palace. But in 1887, largely due to the American interests in the islands, Kalakaua was forced to sign into law a new constitution, surrendering most of the king's governing powers to the legislature of the kingdom.

In 1891, King Kalakaua's sister, Queen Liliuokalani acceded to the throne. By then, however, with the rapid growth of Hawaii's sugar industry, American interests in the islands had become deeply entrenched, and in 1892, upon the start of open rebellion, the *USS Boston* landed on the island of Oahu an armed force to protect American interests. A year later, in 1893, a more or less bloodless revolution deposed Liliuokalani, and brought to power, at the head of a provisional government, Sanford B. Dole. The following year, Hawaii was declared a republic by the Hawaiian legislature, and on June 14, 1900, Hawaii was annexed, under the Organic Act, by the United States, and a territorial form of government established.

In 1902, Prince Jonah Kuhio Kalanianaole, born of royal parentage, and the last heir to the throne, became the first Hawaiian delegate elected to the U.S. Congress. Kuhio led the Hawaiian congressional delegation for the next two decades, and despite not having an official vote in the legislature—as Hawaii was only a territory of the United States at the time—he forged important legislation for the betterment of Hawaii and its people, including the landmark Hawaiian

Homesteads Act of 1910 and the Hawaiian Homes Commission Act of 1921, whereby public lands were made available to native Hawaiians for homesteading. He also obtained funding for such important projects as Pearl Harbor, Honolulu's 12,600-acre deep-water port, and in 1919 and 1920, he introduced the first two successive bills for statehood for Hawaii in the House of Representatives. In 1922, however, Kuhio died, at the age of 50.

The events at the turn of the century also highlighted Hawaii's increasing importance to the United States as a strategic western outpost, and in the following years the U.S. government established military bases throughout the islands, a majority of them, however, on Oahu: Pearl Harbor, Schofield Barracks and Wheeler Field, Bellows Air Force Station, the Kaneohe Marine Corps Air Station, and Fort DeRussy, a 42-acre military reserve at Waikiki, acquired in 1904, which has become a rest and recreation center for military personnel. The military, in fact, now occupies virtually a quarter of the island, comprises approximately 13% of the island's population, and accounts for nearly a third of the island's economy.

The early 1900s also saw the beginnings of Hawaii's pineapple industry. Hawaii's first pineapple company was established in Central Oahu, in Wahiawa, in 1901, by James D. Dole, who also owned nearby Lanai, the "Pineapple Island." In 1903, Dole built the first cannery in the islands, also at Wahiawa, and packed more than 1,800 cases of the fruit that year. In the following years, other pineapple companies were founded on the island, notable among them Libby, McNeill & Libby, established in 1909, and the California Packing Corporation, which opened to business some years later, in 1917. The islands' largest pineapple plantations are now on Oahu, in the Leilehua Plateau in the center of the island, with over 36,000 acres planted to the fruit, accounting for nearly $250 million in sales annually.

In the early 1900s, too, Hawaii's first resort development began on the island of Oahu, at Waikiki. The Moana Hotel, the resort's first commercial hotel—which is also the oldest hotel in Hawaii—was built in 1901, at a cost of approximately $150,000, followed, in 1907, by the Halekulani Hotel, which comprised, simply, a beachfront home and five surrounding bungalows. In 1927, of course, immediately after the completion of the Ala Wai Canal—which was built along the northern end of the resort, to alleviate the area's swampy conditions — the Royal Hawaiian Hotel was built, featuring a Spanish-Moorish design and painted pink, and nick-named "the pink palace." However, it was not until the 1950s and 1960s, that Waikiki finally began to blossom into a world-class resort.

During World War II, of course, Oahu became pivotal in America's entry into the war, when, on December, 7, 1941, one of the island's major installations, Pearl Harbor, became the target of the infamous Japanese air attack, launched from a point approximately 200 miles north of Oahu, in which 353 Japanese war planes bombed the harbor— as well as the Schofield base, Wheeler Field and Bellows Airfield— striking with their first torpedoes "Battleship Row"—an area more or less in the center of the harbor, along the east shore of Ford Island— sinking an entire fleet of American battleships: the *Arizona*—the most

History

famous—*Nevada, Vestal, West Virginia, Tennessee, Oklahoma, Maryland, Neosho* and *California.* The 608-foot-long *USS Arizona,* commissioned in 1916, sank in just five minutes, in 40 feet of water, entombing in its hull all 1,102 servicemen on board. In all, 2,335 U.S. military personnel and 68 civilians were killed in the raid, and 29 Japanese planes shot down.

On August 21, 1959, Hawaii finally gained statehood, becoming the 50th state of the nation — the "Aloha State." That same year, the first commercial jet, a Boeing 707, landed in the islands, at Honolulu, greatly reducing travel time from the continental U.S. to Hawaii, to under 4½ hours. This, effectively, signalled the beginning of tourism in Hawaii.

In the following decade, Hawaii's modern tourist era began in earnest. On the island of Oahu, in the 1960s and 1970s, most of the island's resorts were developed, and Waikiki became Hawaii's—and, indeed, the world's—premier beach resort. Waikiki, in fact, in the 1960s, boasted one of the world's largest hotels, the 20-acre 2,542-room Hilton Hawaiian Village, which remains today one of the largest resorts in Hawaii; and in the 1970s, the hotel construction boom continued, with the development of such resorts as the landmark Sheraton Waikiki, Hawaiian Regent, and the $100-million Hyatt Regency. The 1980s and 1990s, of course, witnessed yet more development, of hotels and resorts, luxury condominium complexes and modern shopping malls, largely concentrated in Waikiki. Waikiki, alone, now attracts nearly 4 million visitors annually—Oahu draws an estimated 5.5 million—and has in it more than 170 hotels and condominium complexes, with over 40,000 guest rooms—more than any other island in Hawaii.

Oahu is now positioned as a premier resort destination, with an abundance of excellent hotel and condominium accommodations and restaurants and other visitor facilities, and a wealth of recreational opportunities, including swimming, snorkeling, scuba diving, surfing, windsurfing, sailing, fishing, hiking, camping, horseback riding, beachcombing, helicopter touring, tennis, golf, and more.

OAHU
"The Gathering Place"

Oahu—which, in Hawaiian, means "gathering place"—is the most populous of the Hawaiian islands, with approximately 75% of Hawaii's population—around 850,000 people. It is also the most popular island in Hawaii, drawing more visitors than any other island in the chain—nearly 5.5 million each year. It has on it, besides, Hawaii's largest metropolis, Honolulu, and its most celebrated beach resort, Waikiki, which alone attracts more than 2.5 million visitors annually.

Oahu is the third largest of the Hawaiian islands, 40 miles long and 25 miles wide, encompassing some 608 square miles. It lies largely between two mountain ranges—the Waianae range along its leeward coast, which also boasts the highest point on the island, Mount Ka'ala, with an elevation of 4,020 feet; and the lush Ko'olau mountains along the windward coast, extending from the northern tip of the island to, more or less, the southern tip. Between the mountain ranges lies a pineapple-filled valley, which comprises Central Oahu, and directly above it, the North Shore, a mecca for surfers, and home to the famous "Banzai Pipeline." On the south shore of the island is Honolulu, a city of nearly 400,000, adjoined to its northwest by historic Pearl Harbor and to its southeast by Waikiki and East Honolulu.

Oahu is situated roughly 95 miles southeast of Kauai, or 25 miles northwest of Molokai; from the island of Maui it is approximately 75 miles distant, northwestward. The island can be reached directly by air or sea from the continental United States and several international cities, or on inter-island flights from any of the other Hawaiian islands —Maui, Hawaii, Molokai, Lanai and Kauai. Oahu's main airport is the Honolulu International Airport, located in Honolulu.

Oahu 19

HONOLULU

Honolulu is the state capital, and the largest metropolis in Hawaii. It has a population of nearly 400,000—representing such ethnically diverse groups as Hawaiians, Caucasians, Chinese, Japanese, Filipinos —and is, quite typically, filled with highrises and shopping centers and fed by multi-laned freeways, not unlike other U.S. cities. It is also, we might add, an historic city, with scores of historic monuments and buildings—many of them dating from the mid 1800s, when Honolulu first became the capital of Hawaii—and ancient *heiaus* and other relics, and, most importantly, the country's only royal palace.

The city itself is situated along the southern end of the island, backed by the lush, northwest-southeast Ko'olau mountains and overlooking Mamala Bay, with historic Pearl Harbor to its northwest and Diamond Head Crater, Oahu's most prominent landmark, to the southeast. For the purposes of touring, of course, it can be divided broadly into six areas: downtown Honolulu, which makes up the city center; Chinatown, adjoining to the west of downtown; the area around the city center, which takes in the Punchbowl Crater as well as Bishop Museum farther to the northwest; Waikiki, the famous beach resort, lying to the southeast of the city center; Manoa Valley, an area just to the northeast, and Tantalus which is a little farther to the north.

Downtown Honolulu

A good place to begin your tour of Honolulu, we might suggest, is the city's downtown, in the heart of which, on the lush, 11-acre Palace Grounds—bordered by South King, Richards, Hotel and Likelike streets—stands the glorious Iolani Palace, once the home of Hawaiian royalty. This is the only royal palace in the nation, built in 1882 by King Kalakaua, at a cost of $350,000, and where, in 1895, Queen Liliuokalani, the last Hawaiian monarch, was imprisoned by the provisional government established by the U.S. The palace remained the seat of government, successively for the Republic, Territory and State until 1969. In 1978, Iolani Palace was restored, at a cost of $6 million, and opened to the public.

In any event, Iolani Palace is one of the grandest and most impressive structures in the islands, built from stone, in the Italian Renaissance architectural style, and filled with European-design period furnishings reminiscent of the royal courts of Europe. Highlights of the palace—which can be viewed on the public tours, offered Wednesday to Saturday, 9 a.m. to 2.15 p.m.—include the Grand Hall, with its ornate *koa* staircase and cedar and redwood walls, adorned with portraits of King Kalakaua and other royal personages, both Hawaiian and European; the adjacent Dining Room, with its elegant period furnishings; the King's Library, featuring a large, 19th-century desk and tables and chairs, an antique telephone—one of the first in

20 Oahu

OAHU

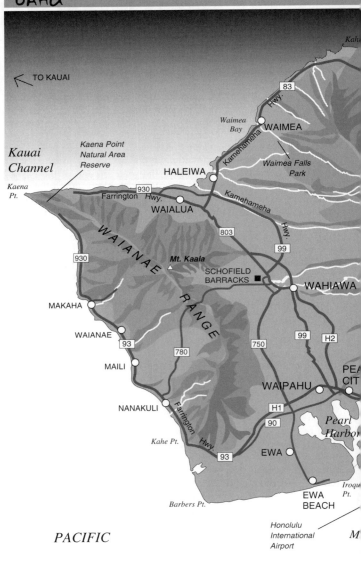

Oahu 21

the islands—and old books and photographs; and the royal bedrooms, of Kalakaua as well as Queen Liliuokalani. Also open to the public is the Throne Room, located on the ground floor and decorated, almost entirely, in red and gold—including the trim, carpets, drapes and furniture upholstery. There are, needless to say, two thrones at one end of the room, for the king and queen. The Throne Room, interestingly, was also the scene, in bygone days, of royal coronations and lavish parties, including the extravagant 50th birthday celebrations for King Kalakaua.

Well worth investigating, too, located adjacent to Iolani Palace are the grey-stone Iolani Barracks, built in 1870, during the reign of Kamehameha V, and where the Royal Guards were housed until the overthrow of the monarchy in 1893. The barracks were originally built on the site of the present-day State Capitol, directly behind the palace on Beretania Street, and moved to their present location in 1965. The statue behind the palace, by the way, facing the State Capitol, is that of Queen Liliuokalani, the last great Hawaiian monarch, who was overthrown in 1893 and who, in 1895, attempted to regain her kingdom, only to be captured and imprisoned in the palace. The 8-foot bronze statue, the work of Boston sculptor Marianne Pineda, was dedicated in 1982.

Also on the palace grounds, of interest to first-time visitors, are the Royal Bandstand-cum-Coronation Stand, which in 1883 provided the setting for the coronation of King Kalakaua and his queen, Kapiolani, and where the Royal Hawaiian Band now performs every Friday; and the site of the Royal Mausoleum and Crypt, originally built here in 1825—for King Kamehameha II and Queen Kamamalu, who died in England in July, 1824—and subsequently relocated, in 1865, to its present site, farther to the north, on Nuuanu Avenue.

Across from Iolani Palace on South King Street, at the corner of Mililani Street, stands Aliiolani Hale, built in 1874 by Kamehameha V—adapted from the original design of Australian architect Thomas Rowe, who, incidentally, also drew up the original plans for the Iolani Palace—to house the Hawaiian parliament and courts. In 1893, however, following the overthrow of the Hawaiian monarchy, the legislature was moved across the street to Iolani Palace, and Aliiolani Hale became the Judiciary Building, which it remains today. The 30-foot bronze statue directly in front of Aliiolani Hale is of course that of Hawaii's first great monarch, Kamehameha I; it is also, we might add, one of Hawaii's most photographed monuments.

Also of interest, located at the corner of Punchbowl and South King streets, is the old Kawaiahao Church, the kingdom's first Christian church, established in 1820 when the first missionaries, led by Hiram Bingham, landed in Hawaii. Bingham, of course, delivered the first sermon in Honolulu on April 25, 1820, and in 1842 he went on to build the Gothic-style church, with 14,000 slabs of coral—some of them weighing more than 1,000 pounds each!—taken from a nearby reef. The church is also significant in that it became the church of Hawaiian royalty, where kings and queens worshipped and were crowned, married, and given their last rites as well. On the grounds, too, in front of the church is the Lunalilo Mausoleum, the final resting

Oahu **23**

place of King Lunalilo, built in 1879.

Adjacent to the Kawaiahao Church on South King Street is the Mission Houses Museum, comprising three historic buildings, dating from the early missionary era and claimed to be the oldest American-style buildings in the islands. The oldest of these, a wood-frame New England-style house, built in Boston in 1821 and shipped around the Horn to Honolulu, has the distinction of being the oldest wooden structure in Hawaii; it originally housed the early missionaries, including Hiram Bingham and Gerrit Judd, and their families. The other two buildings, the Chamberlain House and the Print House, constructed from coral blocks, date from 1831 and 1841, respectively. The Chamberlain House, now fully restored, with period furnishings, was formerly a storehouse for the missionaries; and the Print House, located adjacent to the Chamberlain House, has on display the original, 19th-century printing press on which Elisha Loomis, one of Hawaii's first printers, and the early missionaries printed English-Hawaiian translations of the Bible. All three houses are now open to public viewing.

On South King Street also, at the corner of Punchbowl Street, across from Kawaiahao Church, stands Honolulu Hale—or City Hall—a Spanish Renaissance-style building with a terra-cotta-tiled open courtyard, designed by noted Honolulu architect, C.W. Dickey, and built in 1927; and directly across from there, still at the corner of King and Punchbowl streets, is the Hawaii State Library building, a lovely, early 1900s building with a serene central courtyard, which houses the main branch of the state library system.

Nearby, too, just to the north on Beretania Street, between Punchbowl and Richards streets, is Hawaii's relatively modern State Capitol, built in 1969 at a cost of nearly $25 million. There is a statue of Father Damien, the Belgian priest who devoted much of his life to the lepers on Molokai's remote Kalaupapa Peninsula, directly in front of the State Capitol, and across from there is the state's War Memorial, with a bronze sculptured torch, honoring those who died in World War II.

Also on Beretania Street, a little way from the State Capitol, is Washington Place, a splendid, white colonial mansion, set on landscaped grounds with age-old trees, built in 1847 by a sea captain, John Dominis, whose son, John Owen Dominis, married Lydia Kapa'akea—who later became Queen Liliuokalani. The younger Dominis lived here until his death in 1891, and Liliuokalani, after being deposed in 1893, returned and lived here until her death in 1917. The mansion, originally named for George Washington, is now the official residence of the governor of Hawaii. It is also, quite appropriately, on the National Register of Historic Places.

Another place of interest on Beretania Street, just to the west of Washington Place, at the corner of Alakea Street, is the venerable St. Andrew's Cathedral, featuring cut stones and stained-glass windows imported from England. The Episcopal church was originally founded in 1862 by Kamehameha IV and his wife, Queen Emma, immediately following their visit to Europe, and named for the fact that Kamehameha died on St. Andrew's Day the following year, in 1863.

24 Oahu

DOWNTOWN HONOLULU

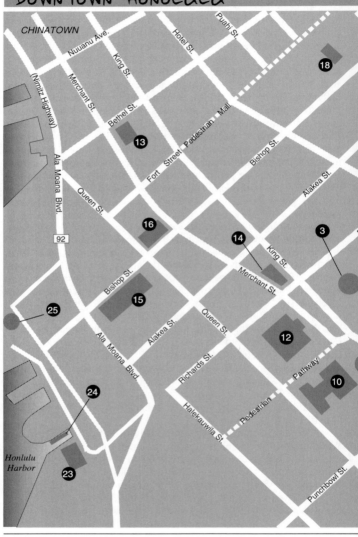

1. Iolani Palace
2. Iolani Barracks
3. Royal Bandstand
4. Queen Liliuokalani Statue
5. Hawaii State Library
6. State Capitol
7. Honolulu Hale (City Hall)
8. Honolulu Municipal Bldg.
9. State Offices Bldg.
10. Aliiolani Hale
11. Kamehameha Statue
12. Old Federal Bldg.
13. Kamehameha V Post Office Bldg.
14. Hawaiian Electric Bldg.
15. Dillingham Bldg.

Oahu

DOWNTOWN HONOLULU

16. Alexander & Baldwin Bldg.
17. Kawaiahao Church
18. Cathedral of Our Lady of Peace
19. St. Andrew's Cathedral
20. Mission Houses Museum
21. Washington Place
22. War Memorial
23. Maritime Museum
24. Falls of Clyde
25. Aloha Tower
26. Honolulu Academy of Arts
27. National Memorial Cemetary of the Pacific (Punchbowl Crater)

Also try to see Our Lady of Peace Cathedral, farther to the west of St. Andrew's on Beretania Street, near Fort Street Mall. The cathedral, constructed from coral blocks taken from a nearby reef and featuring a bell tower, dates from 1840.

Yet another place of interest on Beretania Street, southeastward, a little way, from the State Capitol, between Ward Avenue and Victoria Street, is Honolulu's prestigious Academy of Arts, which houses a splendid collection of both contemporary and ancient art—Oriental, American and European—including works of Gauguin, Van Gogh and Picasso, and Japanese ceramics and paintings, antiques from the Ming and Ching dynasties, and original Hawaiian, South Pacific and even some rare African art. The museum is housed in the former home of Mrs. Montagne Cooke, an avid art collector and founder of the gallery. The building, dating from 1927, features a high peaked, tiled roof, and houses 30 galleries and six delightful garden courtyards with sculptures and abundant native plants. The museum is open to the public, Tuesday to Sunday.

There are, of course, several other buildings of interest in downtown Honolulu, notable among them the Mediterranean-style Old Federal Building on South King Street, located across from the Iolani Palace, dating from 1922 and now housing the U.S. Post Office; the Hawaiian Electric Company building, at the corner of Richards and King streets, built in the 1920s and featuring Spanish-style architecture; the YWCA, situated on Richards Street, on lovely, land-scaped grounds, built in 1926 and designed by noted architect Julia Morgan; and the Italian Renaissance Dillingham Building, located at the corner of Bishop and Queen streets, dating from 1929. Yet more buildings of note include the old Kamehameha V Post Office Building, located at the northeast corner of Merchant and Bethel streets, dating from 1870 and with the distinction of being the first Hawaiian structure built from concrete with reinforced iron bars; the 19th-century Hawaiian Publishing Building, with its ornate trim, located directly across the street from the old post office building; and the Hawaiian-Asian-design Alexander & Baldwin Building at 822 Bishop Street, built in 1929—the work of noted Hawaiian architects C.W. Dickey and Hart Wood—as a memorial to pioneer plantation owners, Samuel T. Alexander and Henry P. Baldwin, founders of the Alexander & Baldwin Corporation, the first of Hawaii's "Big Five" companies.

Chinatown

Honolulu's Chinatown—an area described roughly by Nuuanu Avenue and North Beretania, North King and River streets, encompassing some 38 acres—adjoins immediately to the west of downtown Honolulu. It is, characteristically, a lively, colorful quarter—not dissimilar to Chinatowns in other major cities in the U.S.—with bustling sidewalk markets, scores of Chinese restaurants and diners, noodle factories, fabric outlets and handicrafts emporiums, souvenir shops, and, yes, also a seamy side of town—confined largely to North Hotel Street—dotted with gambling dens, porn shops, dance clubs, pool halls and seedy bars. Chinatown also, we might add, is an historic part of the city, originally established in the early 1800s, following the arrival of the first Chinese immigrants in the late 1700s. The original Chinatown, however, was largely destroyed, and rebuilt, following two devastating fires: the first in 1886, which burned for 3 days, razing nearly eight city blocks, including some 7,000 homes; and the second, the Great Chinatown Fire, which began as a deliberate fire, set by the Board of Health to stem a tide of bubonic plague, but which raged out of control for 17 days, sweeping across nearly 38 acres, engulfing, more or less, the entire Chinatown.

In any case, Chinatown is much to be recommended to first-time visitors to Honolulu, both for its flavor and interest. Here, for instance, you can visit some of Honolulu's most colorful, authentic lei shops—Maunakea Leis, Ala O Hawaii, Sweethearts, Jenny's, Lita's—located along the *makai*—ocean—side of Beretania Street, between Smith and Maunakea streets, and offering a good selection of carnation, plumeria, ginger, pikake, and other fresh floral leis. The shops are quite popular with both visitors as well as Honolulu residents.

Close at hand, too, at the corner of Kekaulike and North King streets, is the old Oahu Market, an institution, no less, originally established in 1904. This is of course one of the liveliest open-air markets in the city, with scores of vendors selling fresh island fish—typically, mahimahi, aku, opakapaka, ono and ahi—and pork, pigs' heads, and a variety of fruit and vegetables, including lychee, starfruit, mangoes, soy beans and bamboo shoots. The market is open daily.

Also of interest to visitors to the area is the historic Wo Fat Restaurant, a Chinatown landmark, and the oldest restaurant in Honolulu, located on North Hotel Street, at the corner of Maunakea Street. Wo Fat, meaning "peace and prosperity," was originally established in 1882, and rebuilt, in its 19th-century Chinese architectural style, with a pink exterior and green tile roof, in 1937, following Chinatown's two major fires in 1886 and 1899.

Another place of interest, situated along Nuuanu Stream, on River Street, between Beretania and Kukui streets, is the River Street Pedestrian Mall, a neglected sort of area, lined with an assortment of Chinese restaurants and diners, which also draws a steady stream of serious players of checkers and mahjongg. There is, by the way, a statue of Sun Yat Sen, founder of the modern Republic of China, located on the mall, at the corner of North Beretania and River streets.

Try to also see the Izumo Taisha Shrine, a traditional Japanese shrine, dating from 1923 and built from wood—without nails—situated on North Kukui Street, directly across from the River Street Pedestrian Mall, on the opposite side of Nuuanu Stream; and the Kuan Yin Temple, with its green tile roofs and red beams, located on North Vineyard Boulevard, near the north end of the mall. This last, the Kuan Yin Temple, is believed to be the oldest Chinese temple in Honolulu, established in the 1880s.

The Honolulu Waterfront

Honolulu's waterfront, largely the section from Aina Moana Beach Park—which lies just to the west of Waikiki—northwestward to the Honolulu Harbor, also has some visitor interest. Here, for instance, at the southeast end of the Honolulu Harbor, at Pier 9, stands the Aloha Tower, a landmark for those arriving or departing Honolulu by ship. The 10-story tower was originally built in 1921, and now houses the offices of the harbor control agency. There is also an Observation Deck here, on the tenth floor of the tower, which is open to the public and can be reached by taking the escalator to the second floor of the pier, then the Observation Elevator to the very top. The Observation Deck, needless to say, offers sweeping views of the city and harbor.

Nearby, too, at Pier 7 at the Honolulu Harbor is the Hawaii Maritime Center, which has in it a maritime museum, devoted largely to ocean travel, with displays of canoes, replica ships, and sailing vessels. There are also exhibits centered around Polynesian history, Hawaiian customs and culture, the Hawaiian sandalwood trade, and the history of whaling, highlighted by 19th-century whaling artifacts and the skeleton of a Humpback Whale. However, the chief attractions here are perhaps the *Falls of Clyde*, a 266-foot, four-masted, square-rigged 19th-century ship, built in Scotland in 1878, and used to transport passengers from San Francisco and the islands, and, later on, also as an oil tanker; and the *Hokulea*, a 65-foot, double-hulled voyaging canoe, built in 1976 as a replica of the ancient ocean-faring canoes, to educate children in the early-day navigational methods used by the first Polynesians to reach the Hawaiian islands. The *Hokulea*, by the way, has made four voyages across the Pacific, from Hawaii to Tahiti, Raiatea and Rarotonga, and back to Hawaii—a 5,500 mile journey—navigating by the stars and the movements of the sea—without the use of tables, charts or any navigational instruments!

Southeastward from the Maritime Center a little way, on Ala Moana Boulevard, between Piikoi and Atkinson streets, is the Ala Moana Shopping Center, Hawaii's largest shopping mall, with over 200 shops, including major department stores such as Sears and Liberty House, scores of boutiques, and a food court with an assortment of ethnic fast-food restaurants.

Also of interest, on the *makai*—ocean—side of Ala Moana Boulevard and the Ala Moana Shopping Center, is the Ala Moana Beach Park, a popular, 77-acre recreation park, with a mile-long, wide sandy beach, visited by nearly 4 million people each year. Swimming is generally safe here, with a protective reef just offshore; besides which, the beach has on-duty lifeguards, tennis courts and a softball field nearby, a snack bar, and showers and restrooms.

Close at hand, too, located at the east end of the Ala Moana Beach Park is the Aina Moana Beach Park—or "Magic Island"—a 36-acre man-made peninsula that jutts out into the Ala Wai Canal, created in 1964. The park has a large grassy area with shade trees

Oahu 29

and, at the tip of the peninsula, a lagoon with a protected, crescent-shaped sandy beach which offers good, safe swimming conditions, a lifeguard on duty, picnic tables, and showers and restroom facilities.

Around Town

Honolulu, besides its downtown, waterfront and Chinatown, has some other places well worth visiting, scattered around town. Notable among them is of course the National Memorial Cemetary of the Pacific, located in the Punchbowl Crater, more or less directly north of the city center, and reached on Puowaina Drive which can be accessed, indirectly, from either the Pali Highway (61) or Lunalilo Freeway (H1). The memorial occupies some 112½ acres on the floor of the Punchbowl Crater—a 75,000-year-old extinct volcano, known, in Hawaiian, as Puowaina, meaning "hill of offering" or "hill of sacrifice," and where, in ancient times, *kapu* breakers were in fact sacrificed at the altar of a *heiau*.

In any case, the National Memorial Cemetery, dedicated in 1949, has in it 28,000 graves of military personnel killed in the Pacific theater in World War II and the Korean War, including that of Ernie Pyle, a well-remembered World War II correspondent who was killed by a sniper on a Pacific island. The memorial also has in it a marble-walled monument, the "Garden of the Missing," with a sweeping flight of steps leading up to it. The marble walls are inscribed with the names of more than 28,000 men and women who served in the South Pacific during World War II and the Korean and Vietnam wars, but whose remains were not recovered or who were missing in action or buried at sea; while a back panel of the memorial depicts the important battles of the Pacific, including Pearl Harbor, Midway, Solomons, Okinawa, Tokyo and Iwo Jima. There is also a 32-seat chapel here, open to the public.

Northward from the Punchbowl Crater, roughly one and one-quarter miles from downtown on Nu'uanu Avenue, and well worth the trip, is the Royal Mausoleum, an historic state monument, built between 1863 and 1865, and which, most importantly, houses the remains of Kings Kamehameha II, III, IV, V and Kalakaua, as well as Queen Liliuokalani, and their families. Only two Hawaiian monarchs are not represented here: Kamehameha I and King Lunalilo. Kamehameha I, of course, died on his native Big Island of Hawaii, where his bones are believed to be buried in secret caves; and Lunalilo, at his request, lies buried in a tomb at the Kawaiahao Church. In any event, the mausoleum building is itself quite striking, Gothic in architectural style, and shaped like a Latin cross, believed to be the work of one of Hawaii's first professional architects, Theodore Heuck.

Also, west from the Punchbowl Crater a little way, on North Vineyard Boulevard, between Nuuanu Avenue and Nuuanu Stream—which is to say, at the north end of Chinatown—are the lovely Foster Botanical Gardens—a 20-acre tropical botanical garden with more than 4,000 species of tropical plants, flowers and trees from all over the world, including scores of native Asian and South Pacific tropical

HONOLULU

TO PEARL HARBOR

TO KANEOHE

63

9

78

H1

Likelike Hwy.

TO PEARL HARBOR

Dillingham Blvd.

4

H1

King St.

Niuanu Ave.

Pali Hwy.

92

Nimitz Hwy.

Ke'ehi Lagoon

Kapalama Basin

Punc Cre

Mokauea Island

SAND ISLAND

Honolulu Harbor

3

Beretai

King

DOWNTOWN

Queen St.

Kapiolani

B

1

Ala Moa.

2

Mamala

Kewalo Basin

Ala Moana Beach Park

Ainamoana State Park (Magic Island)

Ala H

Bay

N

Miles

0   1   2

1. Aloha Tower
2. Iolani Palace

3. Chinatown
4. Bishop Museum

5. National Memorial Cemetery of the Pacific

Oahu

HONOLULU

TO KAILUA

61

Tantalus

Tantalus Dr.

TANTALUS

Round Top Dr.

Round Top

Manoa

Rd.

Manoa Rd.

MANOA VALLEY

Wilder Ave.

Punahou St.

University of Hawaii (Manoa Campus)

H1

Kalakaua

McCully St.

Ala Wai Canal

Kalakaua Ave.

Date St.

Kapahulu Ave.

Waialae Ave.

H1

TO HANAUMA BAY

72

WAIKIKI

Monsarrat Ave.

KAHALA

Kahala Ave.

Kapiolani Park

Diamond Head Crater

DIAMOND HEAD

Diamond Head Rd.

Kupikipikio (Black Point)

6. Paradise Park
7. Lyon Arboretum
8. Queen Emma Summer Palace
9. Moanalua Gardens
10. Royal Mausoleum State Monument

trees, such as the Bo Tree, Chinese Banyan Tree, Tropical Almond Tree, Loulu Palm, Yoke-Wood Tree, Queensland Kauri Tree and Pili Nut Tree, among others. The gardens were originally established in 1855 by German botanist William Hillebrand, and further developed, between 1867 and 1930, by Captain Thomas Foster and his wife, for whom they are named. The gardens are open to the public daily.

Northwest from the Foster Botanical Gardens, approximately one and one-half miles, on Bernice Street—which goes off Likelike Highway (63), which, in turn, can be accessed from the all-important Lunalilo Freeway (H1) northwestward—there is yet another place of supreme interest: the Bishop Museum. The Bishop Museum is Hawaii's most famous museum, frequently referred to as the "Smithsonian of the Pacific," which houses one of the world's greatest collections of Hawaiian cultural and natural history artifacts. It was originally founded in 1889 by Charles Reed Bishop, in memory of his wife, Bernice Pauahi Bishop, a Hawaiian princess from the Kamehameha dynasty, who personally collected many of the artifacts now on display, especially items that once belonged to members of Hawaii's royal families. The museum's chief interest, of course, lies in its Hawaiian Hall, built in 1903 and devoted entirely to Hawaiian history, with its exhibits including, among others, 26 original feather cloaks belonging to the kings of the Kamehameha dynasty—including those worn by Kamehameha I, Hawaii's first great monarch—as well as feather helmets and leis, carved calabashes and wooden tikis, temple drums, 19th-century Hawaiian weapons, royal thrones and royal crowns, and even an original Hawaiian thatched house. There are also several collections of archaeological artifacts unearthed in other South Pacific islands, highlighting the history and culture of Pacific Polynesia; and in the Hall of Hawaiian Natural History, you can view displays of Hawaii's geological formation, including exhibits depicting lava tubes and the region's volcanic ecosystems. In the adjacent Hall of Discovery, housed in a separate building, there is a variety of hands-on educational exhibits for children, centered around science and the culture of the Pacific. The museum, besides, has a planetarium and other separate facilities featuring craft demonstrations, including lei making, hala weaving and quilting, and Hawaiian music and *hula* presentations.

Tantalus

Tantalus—also known as Pu'u Ohia, meaning "ohia tree hill"—is a lush, wild sort of area, high above the city of Honolulu, centered around the Tantalus Mountain, a volcanic peak with an elevation of 2,013 feet. It lies more or less directly northeast of downtown Honolulu, some 3 miles or so, reached by way of a combination of roads—principally, Makiki Drive and Makiki Heights Drive—that eventually emerge on Tantalus Drive or Round Top Drive—the area's two main roads which, together, circle and loop through the area—through a tropical rain forest and groves of bamboo, eucalyptus and banyan trees—with sweeping views of greater Honolulu and the valleys below, offering motorists a most scenic drive.

Tantalus' principal lure is of course its abundant walking trails, quite interesting to outdoor enthusiasts, and ideal for exploring the area. Notable among the nature trails are the Kanealole Trail, which sets out from the top end of the Division of Forestry and Wildlife baseyard, off Makiki Heights Drive, and journeys alongside the Kanealole Stream, passing through lush vegetation and past banana and guava trees and native ginger plants; and the Maunalaha Trail, which begins at the same point as the Kanealole Trail, then follows along the opposite—east—side of the Kanealole Stream from the Kanealole Trail, through a section of a tropical forest overgrown with eucalyptus and bamboo, offering, as an added bonus, views of Honolulu and the valley below. Among other trails here—which go off Tantalus Drive, two or three miles north of the intersection of Makiki Heights Drive—are the Makiki Valley Trail, a short, one-mile trail that passes through the Makiki Valley, crossing over a series of streams and meandering through groves of eucalyptus and kukui nut trees; the Manoa Cliffs Trail, a well maintained trail that snakes around Tantalus Mountain and its cliffs, offering superb views of Manoa Valley, and which also has alongside it several varieties of botanical plants and trees—most of them tagged for easy identification—including hibiscus, and mountain apple and *koa* trees; and the Pu'u Ohia Trail, which traverses Tantalus Mountain, passing by various ferns and trees—including eucalyptus, Norfolk Pine, guava and bamboo—and offers, from the summit, views of Nu'uanu Valley and the island's Windward Coast. There is also a loop trail, the Makiki Valley Loop Trail, which is essentially a combination of the Kanealole, Makiki Valley and Maunalaha trails, but well worth exploring.

Tantalus, besides its hiking trails, also has one or two places to interest the first-time visitor to the area. On Makiki Heights Drive, for one, stands the Contemporary Museum, housed in the former home of Mrs. Montagne Cooke—who, interestingly, also donated her previous home, on Beretania Street, to the Honolulu Academy of Arts -- built in 1926. The museum, which opened in 1988, houses a small, permanent collection of contemporary art—post World War II—as well as changing exhibits. Of particular interest here is British artist David Hockney's vivid, multi-colored three-dimensional environmental exhibit, inspired by Maurice Ravel's 1925 opera, *L'Enfant et les Sortileges*. The museum is open daily, except on Mondays.

Another, the Pu'u Ualaka'a State Wayside Park, a hillside park at an elevation of 1,050 feet, situated off Round Top Drive, some 2½ miles from the intersection of Makiki Drive, is also well worth investigating. Interestingly, the hill upon which the park is situated, now known as Round Top, was originally named Pu'u Ualaka'a— meaning "rolling sweet potato hill"—named for the fact that sweet potatoes were once grown on its slopes and, during harvest time, rolled down the hill for gathering. The park, in any case, offers good picnicking possibilities, and panoramic views of Honolulu and the Pacific Ocean.

Manoa Valley

The Manoa Valley lies just to the east of Tantalus, which is to say, northeast of the city center, some 3 or 4 miles distant, and reached, more or less directly, on Manoa Road. The valley itself is quite large and pictureque, once filled with fields of taro, and where, we are told, Queen Ka'ahumanu, the favorite wife of Kamehameha I, also maintained a vacation home in the 1800s. It is, of course, now dotted with upscale neighborhoods for the most part.

For visitors to the valley, there is the Lyon Arboretum, located on Manoa Road. It is a 124-acre eden of sorts, situated deep in the Manoa Valley, with the lush Koolau Mountains as a backdrop. It was originally established as a forestry nursery in 1918 by Harold L. Lyon, for whom it is named, and is now owned and maintained by the nearby University of Hawaii at Manoa. The arboretum features over 5,000 species of indigenous plants, flowers and trees, including a variety of palms, taro, ginger, heliconia and Malaysian rhododendrons, among others. There is a self-guided tour of the arboretum available to visitors, which leads past the flora and, also, to "Inspiration Point," from where you can enjoy good, all-round views of Manoa Valley and an overview of the arboretum.

There are also one or two good walking trails in the valley, much to be recommended to hikers and nature lovers. The Manoa Falls Trail, a short, three-quarter-mile trail that heads out from the end of Manoa Road, some 3 miles north of Honolulu, is one of the island's most popular trails. It passes through lush, tropical vegetation, including native *ti* plants, eucalyptus, and mountain apple and guava trees, to finally lead to a 100-foot waterfall, at the bottom of which there is a small pool, ideal for splashing around in. Another, the Aihualama Trail, goes off the Manoa Valley Trail, some 50 feet before reaching the Manoa Falls, then journeys roughly one and one-half miles to the Pu'u Ohia and Manoa Cliffs trails junction, passing by groves of bamboo and banyan trees, and through a *koa* forest.

Pali Highway

A worthwhile detour for Honolulu visitors is the Pali Highway (61), which sets out northeastward from Honolulu, approximately 11 miles to the Windward Coast—to Kailua and Kaneohe, bedroom communities of Honolulu in many ways. The highway, nevertheless, is quite scenic, and it has on it one or two places of particular interest to visitors. Just a mile or so from Honolulu, for instance, situated on the southeast—right—side of the highway, is the lovely Queen Emma Summer Palace, a white, colonial mansion, originally built in New England in 1847, and shipped to Hawaii and re-erected. Queen Emma, of course, as students of Hawaiian history will recall, was the wife of Kamehameha IV, who inherited the home from her uncle, John Young II—son of John Young, an adviser to Kamehameha I. In any case, the summer home is now fully restored, and houses the original, antique *koa* furniture, portraits of the Hawaiian royal family, including those of the young prince, Albert, who died at the tender age of 4, and displays of Hawaiian artifacts, among them old feather caps, cloaks, and *tapa* bedspreads. There is also a gift shop on the premises.

Northeastward from the Queen Emma Summer Palace, another half mile, the scenic Nu'uanu Pali Drive goes off the highway to the right—northeastward—and journeys through some splendid, forested areas, re-emerging on the highway a mile or so along. There is a worthwhile short walk here, too, the Judd Trail, which can be accessed from the parking lot on the Nu'uanu Pali Drive, and which follows alongside the Nu'uanu Stream and past groves of ironwoods, eucalyptus and banyan trees.

Farther still, a little way from the north end of Nu'uanu Pali Drive, on the Pali Highway, is the Nu'uanu Pali Lookout, at an elevation of nearly 1,200 feet, and flanked by dramatic cliffs that rise vertically, 2,000 to 3,000 feet. Interestingly, this is also the site of a fierce battle, fought in 1795, between the warriors of Kamehameha I—some 16,000 strong—and the defenders of the island of Oahu, who, during the course of the battle, were driven into the Nu'uanu Valley and, eventually, over these cliffs, to their deaths. The lookout, nevertheless, offers sweeping views of the Windward Coast—quite dramatic with the Ko'olau mountains descending into lush, emerald valleys, and onward to the ocean—and the coastal communities of Kailua and Kaneohe.

From the lookout, it is another 5 miles, approximately, to Kailua, with the highway descending rapidly nearer to the coast.

An alternative route from Honolulu to Kailua-Kaneohe is by way of the Likelike Highway (63), a well-traveled commuter highway, which runs more or less parallel to the Pali Highway, to its north, passing through the Wilson Tunnel, then descending steeply into Kaneohe, with good views of the Kaneohe Bay and the windward coastline.

WAIKIKI

Waikiki is one of the most celebrated beach resorts in the world, and practically synonymous with Hawaii. It lies just to the southeast of downtown Honolulu, along a 2-mile stretch of glorious white sand —which has been divided into a series of beach sections over the years, each with a distinctive name—on the south coast of the island. The resort has a resident population of around 25,000, and is visited by over 2.5 million people each year. It also has some of the most dazzling highrise hotels in the islands, most of them lined along the beach, among them, the well-known Hyatt, Hilton and Sheraton, and more than 20 Outrigger hotels. Besides which, Waikiki offers excellent shopping and dining possibilities—with several good shopping centers, import and souvenir shops, international boutiques, art galleries, and an array of restaurants, representing virtually every known cuisine—

as well as a variety of entertainment, including several celebrity shows.

Waikiki is also one of Hawaii's oldest resorts, which became a favorite recreation spot for Hawaiian royalty in the early 1800s, dotted, along its shoreline, with royal beach houses. In 1901, of course, the resort's first commercial hotel, the Moana Hotel, was built, at a cost of approximately $150,000, followed, in 1907, by the Halekulani Hotel, which comprised, quite simply, a beachfront home and five surrounding bungalows. In 1927, immediately after the completion of the Ala Wai Canal—which was built along the northern end of the resort, to alleviate the area's swampy conditions—the Royal Hawaiian Hotel was built, featuring a Spanish-Moorish design and painted pink, and nick-named "the pink palace." In the late 1950s and 1960s, development of the area began in earnest, with the construction of the grand Hilton Hawaiian Village—the largest hotel in Hawaii—and the Kaiulani and Surfrider hotels, among others; and in the 1970s, 1980s and 1990s, yet more development occurred, with the number of hotel units multiplying from 1,415 in 1950 to 21,217 in 1970, 34,334 in 1980, and 37,270 in 1990. There are now, in fact, more than 170 hotels and condominium complexes in Waikiki, with nearly 40,000 guest rooms!

In any event, Waikiki is strung along a northwest-southeast strip, accessed from downtown Honolulu on Beretania Street—or Lunalilo Freeway or Ala Moana or Kapiolani boulevards—and Kalakaua Avenue, Waikiki's main street, which runs through the heart of the resort. At its northwest end, of course, stand the Hawaii Prince and Ilikai hotels, situated directly across from each other, off Hobron Street —which goes off Ala Moana Boulevard, southward—overlooking the Ala Wai Yacht Harbor. The Hawaii Prince, a 447,000-square-foot 521-room hotel, built in 1990, at a cost of around $150 million, features two 32-story towers, accented with rose-colored glass, with all its rooms looking out over the ocean; and the 800-room Ilikai Hotel, located just to the east of the Hawaii Prince, features three hotel towers and Waikiki's only full-fledged tennis center.

A little way from the Hawaii Prince and Ilikai hotels, eastward, on Kalia Road, is the sprawling, 20-acre 2,542-room Hilton Hawaiian Village, the largest hotel in Hawaii. The resort, recently renovated, in 1988, at a cost of $100 million, comprises 4 hotel towers, with over 100 shops and boutiques, 9 restaurants and 13 cocktail lounges, a convention facility with a 5,000-person capacity, 2 large pools—including a 10,000-square-foot 2-tier pool with waterfalls—a tropical lagoon, a marina, a 6-story 1,800-car parking garage, and Waikiki's largest showroom, the Hilton Dome. The resort, by the way, fronts on the Duke Kahanamoku Beach, palm fringed and with a gently sloping sandy bottom, which has safe swimming conditions year-round, and an on-duty lifeguard. The beach is of course named for Hawaii's champion surfer and swimmer, Duke Kahanamoku, who won the gold medal in the 100-meter freestyle swimming at the 1912 Olympic Games.

Adjoining to the east of the Hilton Hawaiian Village, located along Kalia Road, between Ala Moana Boulevard and Saratoga Avenue, is Fort DeRussy, a large, 42-acre military reserve, largely a grassy

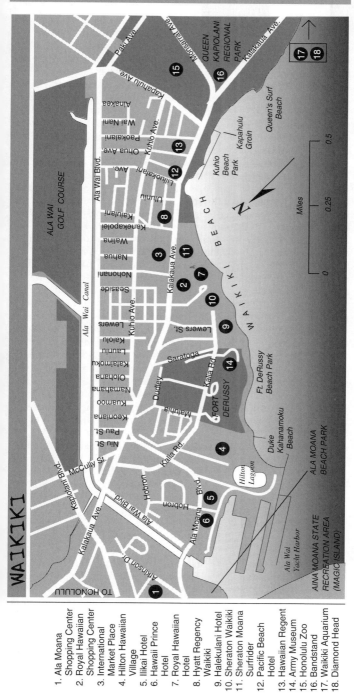

tract, originally acquired by the U.S. government in 1904, and used as a rest and recreation center for military personnel since. There is a museum here, the U.S. Army Museum, located on Kalia Road and housed in the former Battery Randolph structure, which was originally built between 1908 and 1911, to house a battery equipped with 14-inch guns with a range of 14 miles—designed to defend Pearl Harbor and the Oahu coastline. The battery, nevertheless, was dismantled in 1946, after World War II, and in its place, some years later, in 1976, the museum opened. Museum displays are of military exhibits, centered around the history of the U.S. military in Hawaii and the Pacific. The museum is open to public viewing.

Also at Fort DeRussy, directly in front of the U.S. Army Museum, is the Fort DeRussy Beach Park, the largest beach section at Waikiki —nearly 100 yards. The beach, quite naturally, is backed by the grassy Fort DeRussy tract, and palm trees, and it offers, besides, good, safe swimming conditions year-round. The beach also has a lifeguard on duty, and picnic tables, showers and restroom facilities.

Eastward, a little way from Fort DeRussy, and also accessed from Kalia Road, is the Halekulani Hotel, which, in fact, comprises a 5-acre estate with a refurbished beachfront home and five surrounding bungalows—all built in the Hawaiian Monarch style, featuring Italian terrazzo and handcrafted wooden walls—nestled amid landscaped courtyards and tropical gardens. Halekulani—which, in Hawaiian, means "house befitting heaven"—was originally developed as a resort and opened to the public in 1907, and one of the resort's buildings, the "House Without a Key," was later glamorized in one of author Earl Derr Biggers' novels about Charlie Chan. The hotel, interestingly, features an open-air lobby, and gift and specialty shops. The small, sandy beach bordering on the Halekulani resort, by the way, is Gray's Beach, quite popular with serious swimmers, but without any facilities; it does, however, have a public access, leading from Kalia Road, between the Halekulani and Outrigger Reef hotels, and down to the beach.

East of Halekulani, and accessed from Kalakaua Avenue, Waikiki's main thoroughfare, is yet another Waikiki landmark—the grand, 30-story, 1,834-room beachfront Sheraton Waikiki Hotel, situated more or less in the center of Waikiki. The Sheraton Waikiki was originally built in 1971—claimed to be the largest hotel in the world at the time—and renovated, over a period of some five years, between 1982 and 1987, at a cost of around $50 million. The hotel now has in it, among other facilities, 2 pools and 7 full-service restaurants.

Nearby, just east of the Sheraton Waikiki, and also off Kalakaua Avenue, is the historic Royal Hawaiian Hotel, displaying a Spanish-Moorish style of architecture, with a pink exterior, and famous—with good reason—as "The Pink Palace." The hotel was originally built in 1927, at a cost of $4 million, on a 10-acre oceanfront estate with a royal coconut grove, where Queen Ka'ahumanu—King Kamehameha I's favorite wife—once had a summer cottage. During World War II, of course, the hotel was used as a rest and recreation center for U.S. Navy personnel, reopening immediately after the war, in 1947, follow-

Oahu

39

ing a $2 million renovation, as a public hotel once more. In 1992, the hotel was renovated yet again, at a cost of nearly $10 million, and repainted in its traditional "Royal Hawaiian Pink"—using, on its exterior alone, more than 7,000 gallons of the paint! In any case, the "Pink Palace" boasts among its guests President Franklin D. Roosevelt, Shirley Temple, Mary Pickford, Douglas Fairbanks, Clark Gable, and, among the more recent, Kevin Costner, Michael Caine and Rosanna Arquette.

Close at hand, too, on Kalakaua Avenue, at the corner of Royal Hawaiian Avenue, and also well worth visiting, is the Royal Hawaiian Shopping Center, Waikiki's largest shopping center, three blocks long, and with three levels of shops—gift shops, boutiques, art galleries and jewelry shops, among others—and restaurants. There are, in fact more than 150 stores and restaurants in the complex. Another, the International Marketplace, also on Kalakaua Avenue—on the north side of the street—between Dukes Lane and Kaiulani Avenue, is much to be recommended to the first-time visitor as well. It is, after all, Waikiki's original shopping mall, filled, again, with an assortment of shops, galleries, clothing stores, jewelry stands, and restaurants. Both the Royal Hawaiian Shopping Center and International Marketplace are open daily, 9 a.m.-10 p.m.

Just to the east of the Royal Hawaiian Shopping Center, on the ocean side of Kalakaua Avenue, and of particular interest to Waikiki visitors, is the Sheraton Moana Surfrider, Waikiki's oldest hotel—frequently referred to as the "First Lady of Waikiki—dating from 1901 and now a designated historical landmark, listed on the National Register of Historic Places. The original hotel building—a 4-story, colonial-style building—boasted 75 rooms, increasing, by 1918, to 275, with the addition of two newer wings that enclosed a courtyard, at the center of which stood a splendid banyan tree—which has since grown, to a height of nearly 75 feet, with a branch spread of 150 feet or more—planted in 1885; the Banyan Courtyard, of course, as Hawaiian music afficionados will recall, hosted the popular radio show, "Hawaii Calls," from 1935 until 1975. In any event, the hotel now boasts 390 rooms—only 130 of which are located in the original 4-story Moana Hotel building—and 4 restaurants and bars, including the Banyan Tree Bar, quite possibly one of the best beach bars in Waikiki.

Across the street from the Surfrider, and adjacent to the International Marketplace—on Kaiulani Avenue, at the corner of Kalakaua Avenue—stands the Princess Kaiulani Hotel, one of Waikiki's first highrises, built in 1955, with an 11-story tower. The hotel, however, has greatly expanded since, adding two new wings, including a 28-story tower completed in 1970, and now has a total of 1,150 guest rooms, several restaurants and bars, tropical gardens, gift and specialty shops on the premises, a pool, and an open-air hotel lobby. Interestingly, the hotel is named for Princess Victoria Kaiulani, born in 1875 and anointed heir apparent by Queen Liliuokalani—the last Hawaiian monarch and aunt to Kaiulani—in 1891.

Across from the Princess Kaiulani Hotel, on the east side of Kaiulani Avenue and fronting on Kalakaua Avenue, is the splendid,

1,230-room Hyatt Regency Waikiki, a luxury hotel, no less, developed in 1976 by Hawaii's famous developer, Chris Hemmeter, at a cost of around $100 million. The hotel itself comprises twin 40-story towers, built on either side of a delightful, 10-story atrium—known as the "Great Hall"—which features three cascading waterfalls—one to three stories high—abundant lush, tropical plants, and several exotic and native birds; there is also a pool deck here, more than 70 shops and boutiques, and no fewer than eight well-appointed restaurants and bars, many of them offering live entertainment. There is, besides, a sandy beach directly across from the hotel, just over Kalakaua Avenue, with good swimming and surfing possibilities, and a lifeguard station, surfboard rental concession, showers and restroom facilities.

Also of interest, a little way from the Hyatt Regency, south-eastward along Kalakaua Avenue, are the Pacific Beach Hotel and the Hawaiian Regent Hotel, with 850 and 1,350 rooms, respectively. The Pacific Beach Hotel also has a pool, tennis courts, and a 3-story-high, 280,000-gallon oceanarium which features daily feedings at 9 a.m., noon, and 1.30, 5.30, 7 and 8.15 p.m.; and the Hawaiian Regent, for its part, boasts six superb restaurants, two pools, a shopping arcade, and an open-air lobby and courtyard featured in the TV series, *Magnum P.I.*

South of Kalakaua Avenue, directly across from the Pacific Beach and Hawaiian Regent hotels, between Liliuokalani and Kapahulu avenues, lies Kuhio Beach Park, one of the finest beach sections at Waikiki, named, quite appropriately, for Hawaii's favorite son Prince Jonah Kuhio Kalaniana'ole—nephew of Queen Kapiolani and, later on, one of Hawaii's first delegates to the United States Congress—who once had a home here. At the beach, at its western end, you can search out the Kapahulu Groin, a storm drain that extends south-westward from Kapahulu Avenue into the ocean, quite popular with boogie boarders; and the "wall," which is essentially a retaining wall that runs northwestward from the Kapahulu Groin, parallel to the shoreline, enclosing in it one or two pools which offer good swimming possibilities. The beach also has a lifeguard on duty, and showers.

Adjoining to the southeast of Kuhio Beach Park is the Kapiolani Beach Park, another well-liked beach section that extends southeast-ward from the Kapahulu Groin to the Natatorium War Memorial — located adjacent to the Sans Souci Recreation Area. The beach, at its western end, near the Kapahulu Groin, is rather narrow, bordered by clusters of coral and lava rock; but it soon fans out, nearer the center, into a lovely, wide section, known as the Queen's Surf Beach, quite popular with gays, and which has a sandy bottom and is bordered, to its north, by a large, grassy area, palm fringed and dotted with picnic tables. The beach also has a lifeguard station, and showers and rest-rooms.

Inland from the Kapiolani Beach, of course, lies the Kapiolani Park, encompassing some 100 acres, and with the distinction of being Hawaii's first public park, dedicated in 1877, to Queen Kapiolani, wife of King Kalakaua. The park, once the site of a race track, is now one of the most popular recreation areas in greater Honolulu, ideally suited to picnicking, jogging, kite flying, and the like. It also has in it, among other facilities, four tennis courts with lights, a bandstand, the Waikiki Shell amphitheater, the Honolulu Zoo, the Waikiki Aquarium, and a small, stadium-like area for the Kodak Hula Show. The park itself is largely grassy, dotted with palms, ironwoods and banyan trees.

The Honolulu Zoo, located in the Kapiolani Park and accessed from Kapahulu Avenue—which goes northward off Kalakaua Avenue —is Hawaii's largest and best-kept zoo, with over 1,000 typical zoo animals, such as monkeys, elephants, giraffes and tigers, and a variety of indigenous and exotic tropical birds. It also features a "Reptile House" which has in it some of Hawaii's only snakes—since there are no snakes on the islands—and the "African Savannah," where you can see African animals—some 200 animals native to east Africa —in natural settings. Among other special attractions at the zoo are the Petting Zoo, quite interesting to children, and the "Elephant Encounter"—featured at 11 a.m. daily—in which, in close proximity to the animals, you can learn all about elephants. The zoo is open daily, 8.30 a.m. to 4.30 p.m.

Also at Kapiolani Park, in a lawn area near the bandstand, the colorful Kodak Hula Show is staged—a popular event, which began in 1937, and which features, quite typically, a live Hawaiian band—made up of older Hawaiian women in *mu'umu'us* and floppy hats, playing *ukuleles*—offering traditional Hawaiian music, and an authentic *hula* performance, with several native Hawaiian women dancers, wearing bright floral leis and grass and ti leaf skirts. The show is held three times each week, on Tuesdays, Wednesdays and Thursdays, with stadium-type seating for spectators. The show is offered to the public free of charge, and provides some good opportunities for amateur photographers.

Another place of interest at the park, well worth investigating, is the Waikiki Aquarium, accessed from Kalakaua Avenue. The Waikiki Aquarium is an excellent small aquarium, with several good exhibits, including display tanks of reef sharks, turtles, Hawaiian monk seals, rays, octopi, a seahorse, giant clam, live coral, and even deep-sea chambered nautilus. There is also a pool here, which simulates a coral reef, offering visitors the unique experience of learning all about reef life first hand.

Farther still, along Kalakaua Avenue, between the Waikiki Aquarium and the Sans Souci State Recreation Park, is the Natatorium War Memorial, with its large stone facade, built in 1927, as a memorial to island men who fought in World War I. There is also a 100-meter salt-water pool near the memorial, on the ocean side of Kalakaua Avenue, just west of the Sans Souci recreation area; it is, however, no longer open to the public for swimming.

Finally, there is the Sans Souci State Recreation Area, a small, sandy beach area, which is also the easternmost and one of the least crowded of Waikiki's beaches, quite popular with vacationing families. Interestingly, in the 1890s, we are told, Sans Souci was also visited by Scottish-born author Robert Louis Stevenson, in his quest for better health. The beach, in any case, has a sandy, gently sloping bottom, and offers good, safe swimming conditions; it also has a lifeguard on duty, and showers and portable toilets. At the beach, too, are the modest,

125-room New Otani Kaimana Beach Hotel, with one or two good restaurants and superb views of the ocean, and two other hotels, quite close to the New Otani—the 21-story 101-room Colony Surf Hotel and the smaller, 53-unit Diamond Head Beach Hotel, both bordering the beach, and with unobstructed views of the ocean.

East of Waikiki, Kalakaua Avenue ends and Diamond Head Road begins, the latter journeying along the south of the Diamond Head Crater, passing directly above the Kuilei Cliffs Beach Park—located approximately three quarters of a mile from Kapiolani Park. Just off Diamond Head Road, above the Kuilei Cliffs Beach, are three successive lookouts—that offer sweeping views of the ocean below—with a paved pathway dashing off down to the beach from near the first of the lookouts, and a plaque of some interest located at the second lookout, dedicated to pioneer aviator Amelia Earhardt, who, aviation buffs will recall, became the first person to fly solo from Hawaii to the mainland, on January 11, 1935. In any event, Kuilei Cliffs Beach is a long, narrow beach, bordered by a coral reef just offshore. Swimming is generally not recommended here, primarily due to the reef.

A little way from the Kuilei Cliffs, Diamond Head Road curves around the Diamond Head Crater, northwestward, until, at the intersection of 18th Avenue, the entrance to the crater is reached. From here, it is another half mile or so to the crater floor and a public parking lot. In any case, Diamond Head is Hawaii's most famous landmark, named for its volcanic crystals—calcite—which early-day Western sailors once mistook for diamonds. The crater itself is more than 100,000 years old, and it has its highest point Leahi, located near the southwest end of the crater rim, with an elevation of 760 feet. There is a three-quarter-mile foot trail that leads from the crater floor to the rim, to Leahi, winding along a series of switchbacks and climbing some 200 steps through two tunnels—all in the dark. The effort, nevertheless, is well worth it, for the lookout at Leahi offers some of the most spectacular views of the Pacific Ocean. Diamond Head Crater, by the way, is also home to the headquarters of the Department of Transportation, the Federal Aviation Administration, and the Civil Defense Emergency Operation Center.

Just around Diamond Head, too, approximately three and one half miles east from Waikiki, on Kahala Avenue—the coastal road that goes off Diamond Head Road, eastward—stands the 10-story 370-room Kahala Hilton Hotel, originally developed in 1964, designed by architect Edward Killingsworth. This is of course one of Oahu's older, established hotels, fronting on a lovely, wide, sandy beach—which has good, safe swimming conditions—and surrounded on its other three sides by the lush, green Waialae Country Club Golf Course. The hotel itself has beautifully landscaped grounds too, abundant in tropical plants and fragrant flowers, and interspersed with tiny waterfalls and delightful little streams. However, the centerpiece of the hotel—and few, if any, will argue otherwise—is its Dolphin Lagoon, home to three bottle-nosed dolphins, and also containing hundreds of reef fish and sea turtles, and two South African black-footed penguins. There are daily shows featuring the dolphins, at 11 a.m., 2 p.m. and 4 p.m. Besides which, the hotel also features, among its entertainers, local

Oahu

43

celebrity Danny Kaleikini, who has headed the nightly Polynesian revue here for more than 25 years.

EAST HONOLULU

East Honolulu, as the name suggests, adjoins immediately to the east of Honolulu and Waikiki, comprising the southeast corner of the island, east from Diamond Head to Makapu'u Point, taking in, for the most part, the coastal stretch along Maunalua Bay—backed by the lush Ko'olau mountains—and Koko Head and Hanauma Bay. this also, we might add, is an increasingly affluent area, with several exclusive residential communities tucked away in the Ko'olau foothills and valleys, just above Maunalua Bay and the Kalanianaole Highway (72), among them Kahala, Aina Haina, Niu Valley, and, most impressive of all, Hawaii Kai, a sprawling subdivision, with extensive waterways and lagoons, situated at the foot of Koko Crater.

East Honolulu, however, is also not without visitor interest. Here, for instance, just east of Diamond Head, 2 to 5 miles distant, are a series of beach parks—Wailupe, Kawaikui, Kuliouou and Maunalua —all quite well liked, strung along Maunalua Bay, and protected from the ocean by a reef that extends some 4 miles, just offshore, more or less along the entire length of the bay. The Maunalua Bay Beach Park, which is situated farthest east—nearly 5 miles east of Diamond Head —has, in addition, a boat ramp, and, naturally, good boating, jet skiing, windsurfing and para-sailing possibilities.

Directly northeast of the Maunalua Beach Park lies Hawaii Kai, the prestigious suburb of East Honolulu, and just to the southeast of there—approximately 7½ miles east of Waikiki, and also reached on Kalanianaole Highway (72)—are the distinctive Koko Head and Hanauma Bay. Koko Head is of course a landmark of sorts, 642 feet high, well rounded, and characteristic in its red soil, named for both its shape and color; and Hanauma, which in Hawaiian means "curved bay," is a lovely, horseshoe-shaped, aquamarine bay, abundant in a variety of marine life, and easily one of the most popular snorkeling spots in the islands. Hanauma Bay, in fact, incorporates in it the Hanauma Bay Underwater Park, a designated marine life preserve, established in 1967. Also of interest, near the head of the bay—at its north end—is Keyhole, a large, sandy-bottom area in the center of a reef that protects the bay from the open ocean, quite popular with swimmers, and which, when viewed from the cliffs directly above, resembles a keyhole. Another place of interest at the bay is the "Toilet Bowl," situated along the east side of the bay, where a small, natural pool fed by underwater lava tubes, rises and falls with the ocean surges, simulating the filling and flushing of a toilet bowl. Hanauma Bay, besides, has also, over the years, provided the setting for such memorable films as *Blue Hawaii*, starring Elvis Presley, and *From Here To Eternity*.

North from Hanauma Bay, approximately three quarters of a mile, is a scenic overlook, from where, on clear days, you can see the island

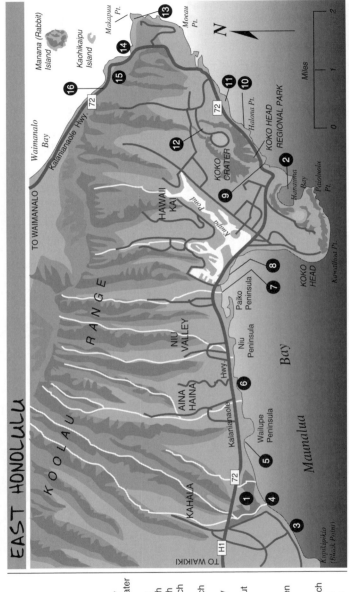

Oahu
45

of Molokai, across the Kaiwi Channel, some 25 miles distant; and another mile or so from there, on the *makai*—ocean—side of the highway (72), is Halona Cove, with a parking lot located just off the highway, and a trail leading down from the west side of the parking lot to Halona Beach—a small, crescent-shaped beach where, by the way, swimming is not advised due to the strong under currents. Also of interest, on the east side of the Halona Cove parking lot, at Halona Point, is the Halona Blowhole, spouting, intermittently, plumes of ocean water. There are also good views from the blowhole, of Sandy Beach, farther up the coast.

Northeastward from Halona Beach, a quarter mile on Kalanianaole Highway, and we are at Sandy Beach, the island's most popular bodysurfing spot, and the site of several bodysurfing contests each year. The beach itself is long and wide, with on-duty lifeguards and showers and restroom facilities, and adjoined by a large, grassy area, ideal for picnicking and kite flying.

Inland from Sandy Beach—to the west of it—lies the Koko Crater, reached by way of Kalanianaole Highway, approximately a quarter mile northward from Sandy Beach, to Kealahou Road, then a little over a half mile northwestward to a dirt road which, in turn, dashes off westward toward the Koko Head Stables, leading, finally—a half mile further—to the crater. Koko Crater is nearly 200 yards wide, and shaped like a horseshoe, home to the Koko Crater Botanical Gardens, which can be seen in various stages of development. Directly above the crater, at its southwest end—on the crater rim—is Pu'u Mai, the highest point in the area, with an elevation of 1,204 feet.

From the Koko Crater, let us return to Kalanianaole Highway, our main route of travel, which proceeds northeast toward Makapu'u Beach, nearly two miles distant. But before Makapu'u Beach, roughly a mile northeast of Sandy Beach, the Makapu'u Lighthouse Trail dashes off the highway (72), seaward, some one and one-half miles, to Makapu'u Point—the easternmost point on Oahu—and the Makapu'u Lighthouse, situated on a cliff above the water, but which, unfortunately, is not open to the public. There are, nevertheless, good, all-round views from here, of the islands of Molokai and Lanai to the southeast, and, on Oahu itself, of the Ko'olau mountains and the Windward Coast.

Finally, below Makapu'u Point, a half mile or so, is Makapu'u Beach Park, a crescent-shaped sandy beach, bordered by coral and backed by shallow sand dunes, quite popular with bodysurfing enthusiasts; and directly across from there, on the opposite side of the highway, is Oahu's Sea Life Park, where you can see, in large tanks and pools, a variety of marine life, including whales, dolphins, sharks, Hawaiian monk seals, sea lions, turtles, penguins, and the world's only "wholphin"—the offspring of a killer whale and a bottlenose dolphin. Among the park's notable attractions are the mammoth Hawaiian Reef Tank, a 300,000-gallon aquarium; the Rocky Shores, an 11,000-gallon exhibit designed to recreate the surf- and wave-swept intertidal zone of Hawaii's shoreline; the Hawaii Ocean Theater, where, in an open amphitheater setting, bottlenose dolphins perform; the Pacific Whaling Museum, which boasts one of the largest collections of whaling artifacts and scrimshaw; and the Whaler's Cove and Lagoon, the Sea Lion Feeding Pool, Seabird Sanctuary, Penguin Habitat, Turtle Lagoon, Shark Gallery, and a children's touch pool. There is also a restaurant on the premises, and live entertainment on the weekends, as well as a sea lion show.

Also of interest, just offshore from Makapu'u Point, are two islands—Manana and Kaohikaipu—both preserved as seabird sanctuaries. The larger of the two islands, Manana Island, also known as Rabbit Island, has on it, for added interest, one or two ancient Hawaiian fishing shrines.

PEARL HARBOR

Pearl Harbor—a 12,600-acre, or 8.5-square-mile, harbor, located just to the northwest of Honolulu, and named for the small pearl oysters found there in abundance in the early 1800s—is Hawaii's most renowned harbor. On December 7, 1941, during World War II, it was the target of a devastating air attack, in which 353 Japanese war planes swooped down on Pearl Harbor, the Schofield military installation, Wheeler Field, and Bellows Airfield, striking with their first torpedoes "Battleship Row"—an area more or less in the center of the harbor, along the east shore of Ford Island—sinking an entire fleet of American battleships: the *Arizona*—the most famous—*Nevada, Vestal, West Virginia, Tennessee, Oklahoma, Maryland, Neosho* and *California*. The *Arizona*, measuring 608 feet in length, and commissioned in 1916, was among the first casualties of the raid, and sank in just five minutes, in 40 feet of water, entombing in its hull all 1,100 servicemen. In all, 2,335 U.S. military personnel and 68 civilians were killed in the attack. It was the "Day of Infamy."

The USS Arizona Memorial, built directly over the sunken ship, and dedicated on May 30—Memorial Day—in 1962, is now the centerpiece and chief visitor attraction of Pearl Harbor, visited by nearly 2 million people each year, and with the distinction of being the most visited sight on the island. There is a Visitor Center located just off Highway 90 and Arizona Memorial Place, where you can view a 20-minute film on the history of the *USS Arizona* and Pearl Harbor, and which also has a museum with some interesting exhibits, including scale models of Pearl Harbor and the battleship prior to the attack, as well as a Japanese torpedo recovered from the harbor only recently, in May, 1991. From the Visitor Center, you can also take a ferry—as part of an organized tour of the memorial—to the gracefully-arched, 184-foot-long white structure in the center of the harbor, built directly over the battleship. At the memorial there is a list of the servicemen entombed in the *Arizona*, and also a viewing area from where you can see, some 7 or 8 feet below, the hull of the *Arizona*.

Also of interest, located more or less adjacent to the USS Arizona Memorial Visitor Center is the US Bowfin Submarine Museum and Park, where you can visit a real, 1,500-ton submarine, the *US Bowfin*.

Oahu **47**

A self-guided tour of the submarine—with pre-taped commentary piped through "sound sticks"—leads through the various sections of the submarine, including the Captain's Room, officers' quarters, sleeping quarters, bunk room, mess-cum-kitchen, torpedo room, engine rooms, and a maneuvering room. There is also a submarine museum, with old photographs and exhibits depicting the history of submarines, and scale models and displays of torpedos, instruments used to determine torpedo angles, depth charges, and authentic control panels. The museum and park are open to the public daily.

Two other places of interest in the Pearl Harbor area, situated a little way to the east and northeast of the harbor, respectively, are the Moanalua Gardens and the Keaiwa Heiau State Recreation Area. The first of these, the Moanalua Gardens—which can be reached by way of Moanalua Road (Highway 78) east from Pearl Harbor, approximately 3 miles, then Puuloa Road northward briefly to Mahiole Street, which leads to the gardens—is a splendid, 26-acre park, with huge monkey pod trees and a lily pond, situated adjacent to the delightful, wooded Moanalua Valley—a haven for nature lovers and hikers. The park, however, also has in it the Royal House of Oahu, an historic summer cottage where King Kamehameha V entertained frequently; and an old Chinese meeting hall, dating from the early 1900s. The park, in addition, offers excellent picnicking possibilities.

The Keaiwa Heiau State Recreation Area, which lies to the northeast of Pearl Harbor, can be reached by following Aiea Heights Drive—which goes off Moanalua Road (Highway 78), 3 miles or so west of the Moanalua Gardens—directly northeastward, ascending some 2½ miles, to the park. The park itself is situated on hill overlooking Pearl Harbor. It is, quite typically, filled with *ti* plants, eucalyptus trees and Norfolk pines, with several enchanting little trails winding through it, including the 4½-mile Aiea Loop Trail. The park's principal attraction, however, is the Keaiwa Heiau, a large, 100-foot-wide and 150-foot-long *heiau*, with low stone walls and platforms. The *heiau*, we are told, was once a medicinal, healing center, where Hawaiian *kahuna*—herb doctors—practised their art of healing. There are still herbs grown in the gardens here, which were once compounded and administered to patients.

CENTRAL OAHU

Northwest of Pearl Harbor lies Central Oahu, made up largely of a pineapple-filled valley that extends northwestward, between the Waianae Mountains and the Ko'olau Range, to Haleiwa and the island's north shore. The principal towns here are of course Pearl City and Waipahu, situated on the periphery of Pearl Harbor—10 miles and 14 miles from downtown Honolulu, respectively—and Wahiawa, a modest-sized town, another 7 or 8 miles further, nestled amid fields of pineapple.

Pearl City and Waipahu are important population centers—an extension of Honolulu in many ways—situated adjacent to one another, and filled with restaurants, shopping centers and other modern facilities. In Pearl City, however, there is little to interest the visitor, although Waipahu, just west of Pearl City, does have a place of interest, well worth investigating, especially for first-time visitors. Here, on Waipahu Street—which goes off Paiwa Street, which, in turn, goes off the all-important H1 freeway, some 12 miles west of Honolulu— you can search out the Waipahu Garden Cultural Park, located more or less in the center of town, directly across from the old Oahu Mill— a 19th-century sugar mill, around which the town of Waipahu, in fact, sprang up. In any case, the cultural park—an historic plantation village and outdoor museum of sorts—encompasses some 50 acres, and was developed only recently, in 1992, at a cost of around $3 million. It features, typically, some 30 replica 19th-century homes and buildings of various ethnic groups from the plantation era, including Hawaiian, Chinese, Portuguese, Puerto Rican, Japanese, Okinawan, Korean and Filipino, all with original, period furnishings. The Chinese Society Building—which has in it a temple—and the Chinese Cookhouse date from around 1909 and are among the oldest wooden structures in Waipahu; the Portuguese House, also a wood-frame structure, features, as its chief attraction, a *forno* (Portuguese bread oven); the Puerto Rico House, again, is a basic wooden house, white-washed and with two rooms and a lanai, dating from 1909; and the Japanese duplex, where you can visit a building directly behind the main house, where tofu was once produced and sold, and an adjacent authentic Japanese Shinto shrine, dating from 1916. Also try to see the Okinawan House, consisting of three structures; the Filipino dormitory, which once housed hen coops and warring rooster pens, and communal dining rooms for its all-male population; a Sumo Ring, 15 feet square, where Japanese immigrants staged sumo wrestling matches for King Kala- kaua during his visits to the compound in 1885; and the old Camp Office which also incorporates in it the plantation store, featuring an antique freezer, presses, stove and table. In the complex, too, is the Hawaiian Hale, a thatched, wooden-post structure, on a coral and lava rock platform, dating from 1840-1876, and once used as living and sleeping quarters for Hawaiian plantation workers.

North from Waipahu on the Kamehameha Highway (99), some 7 miles distant, and situated more or less in the heart of Central Oahu's pineapple-filled valley, is Wahiawa, another old plantation town, bustling with activity, largely supported by military personnel from the adjoining Schofield Barracks. The town, quite typically, is filled with eateries and restaurants, a variety of shops, and, yes, tattoo parlors.

Wahiawa, however, is also not without visitor interest. It has in it, among other places, the Wahiawa Botanical Gardens, a 27-acre botanical garden, located on California Street, which goes off Kameha- meha Highway (99). The garden was originally established as a nursery and experimentation site for sugarcane varieties—owned by the Hawaii Sugar Plantation Association—in 1957. It now features, in a lush setting, flowers, plants and trees from around the world, including several types of spice trees, pandanus trees, bamboo, and native Hawaiian plants. The gardens are open to the public daily, 9 a.m. to 4 p.m.

Also on California Street in Wahiawa, westward a little way from the Wahiawa Botanical Gardens, near the United Methodist Church, are the two ancient "healing stones," sheltered in a concrete shrine, and with a Hawaiian Visitors Bureau marker pinpointing the location of these. The stones are believed to have been part of headstone used at the burial of a once-powerful and influential Hawaiian *ali'i*—chief —and thus bestowed, it is claimed, with magical healing powers—a lure, needless to say, for thousands of visitors each year.

Of interest, too, are the Kukaniloko Birth Stones, reached by way of Kamehameha Highway north from California Street, a half mile or so, to Whitmore Avenue, then left—westward—onto a dirt trail which leads another quarter mile, roughly, to the stones, tucked away in a grove of palms on the north side of the road. This, in any case, is an important birthplace of Hawaiian royalty, where, according to popular belief, mothers of royal lineage would come to give birth to their babies—future kings and queens, no less—for the *ali'i* had declared this to be a sacred place, bestowed with divine powers.

Adjoining to the west of the Wahiawa township, of course, are the Schofield Barracks, a U.S. Army base, home to the 25th Infantry Division, named for Major General John M. Schofield, the army's Pacific military division commander in the the late 1800s. For visitors, however, the place to visit at the Schofield Barracks is the Tropical Lightning Museum, reached by way of the Foote Gate entrance, from where you can follow the main road, roughly three quarters of a mile to the museum, at the corner of Waianae and Kolekole avenues. The museum has several good exhibits, largely centered around the history of the barracks, and also including information and memorabilia from various conflicts, such as World War II, and the Korean and Vietnam wars. Among the displays are an assortment of uniforms, field packs, rifles and machine guns, old photographs, and even an exhibit of bunk inspections. The museum, by the way, is named for the 25th Infantry Division, also known as the "Tropic Lightning Infantry," with a self-professed notoriety to "strike anywhere, anytime."

Northward from Wahiawa, too, on Kamehameha Highway (99), there are one or two places of interest: the Del Monte Pineapple Variety Garden, located at the junction of highways 99 and 80, one and one-half miles from Wahiawa, which has several varieties of pineapple plants on display, from the Bahamas, South Africa, Samoa, Malaya, the Philippines, and Brazil, and also an exhibit centered around the history of pineapple production in Hawaii; and the Dole Plantation, located approximately three-quarters of a mile north of the Del Monte Pineapple Variety Garden on Kamehameha Highway, where, amid fields of golden pineapples, stands a tourist-alluring gift shop, laden with a myriad of fresh fruit and fruit juices, and island souvenirs. There is, by the way, also a variety garden at the Dole Plantation, with sample pineapple plants from around the world.

There remains yet another place of interest in Central Oahu: Ironwood Avenue. This is in fact an alternative route to the North Shore, journeying along a quiet country road—lined with ironwood trees on both sides of the thoroughfare—which runs more or less parallel to the north-south Waianae Mountain Range, treating the motorist-sightseer to several scenic vistas. The "avenue" actually makes up a one-mile section of Highway 803, just north from the intersection of highways 803 and 99—some 4 miles north of Schofield Barracks.

NORTH SHORE

Oahu's North Shore, which makes up the northern portion of the island, from Haleiwa northeastward to Kaihalulu Beach, is practically synonymous with surfing, home to the famous "Banzai Pipeline" and other equally spectacular waves that break just off the coast here, at Sunset Beach, Waimea Bay, and a series of other beaches. This also, we might add, is a popular vacation retreat for island dwellers, with its small country towns and rural atmosphere—quite in contrast to metropolitan Honolulu—and its well-liked beach parks and glorious sunsets, and, most importantly, abundant recreational facilities.

A logical place to begin your tour of the North Shore is of course Haleiwa, the "Gateway to the North Shore," situated at the southwest end of the coastal stretch—at the top end of Kamehameha Highway (99)—the first town to be reached on the North Shore when approaching from Central Oahu. Haleiwa is an old sugar plantation town, small, but, not surprisingly, the largest population center on the North Shore, which once was a commercial and social center of sorts, located, during the early 1900s, at the end of the Oahu Railway & Land Company's railroad, and quite popular with Honolulu visitors. The town is now, for the most part, crammed with an assortment of boutiques, galleries and shops—including several surf shops where you can buy or rent all types of surfboards, wetsuits and other surfing paraphernalia—and health food stores, restaurants and eateries—among them two of the island's most famous "shave ice" stalls, Matsumoto's and Aoki's, where you can sample shave ice—tropical snow cones—in a variety of flavors—coconut, pineapple, banana, papaya, mango, lilikoi—and even shave ice with vanilla ice cream and sweet azuki beans.

Haleiwa, as one would expect, also has in it two or three beach parks. On Haleiwa Road, for one, a quarter mile or so west of Kamehameha Highway—which on the North Shore becomes Highway 83—lies the Haleiwa Ali'i Beach Park. The Haleiwa Ali'i is a large beach—long, wide, and sandy—fronted by formations of coral reef, and with good facilities, including an on-duty lifeguard, picnic tables, showers and restrooms. It is also, we might add, the site of several surfing competitions each year, well-liked for its large winter waves.

Another, the Kaiaka State Recreation Area, is located just to the west of Haleiwa Ali'i Beach Park—at the northeast end of Kaiaka Bay—along Haleiwa Road, approximately a mile distant. The park has in it a small, sandy beach, punctuated with coral, and a sprawling grassy area with a handful of ironwood trees. The park also has some camping possibilities, and picnic tables and restrooms; swimming,

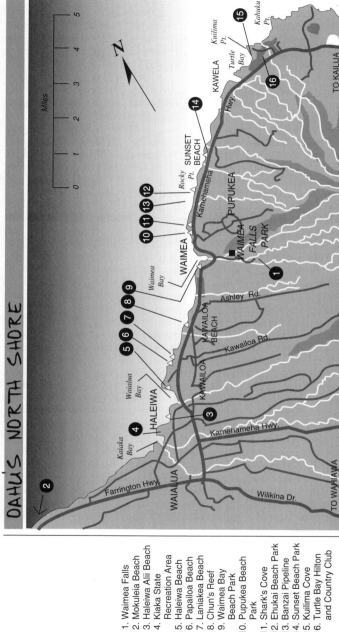

OAHU'S NORTH SHORE

1. Waimea Falls
2. Mokuleia Beach
3. Haleiwa Alii Beach
4. Kiaka State Recreation Area
5. Haleiwa Beach
6. Papailoa Beach
7. Laniakea Beach
8. Chun's Reef
9. Waimea Bay
10. Pupukea Beach Park
11. Shark's Cove
12. Ehukai Beach Park
13. Banzai Pipeline
14. Sunset Beach Park
15. Kuilima Cove
16. Turtle Bay Hilton and Country Club

however, is not advised here due to the strong ocean currents.

Also of interest is the Haleiwa Beach Park, situated just off Kamehameha Highway (83), roughly one and one-half miles northeast of mile marker 0, just over the Anahulu Stream Bridge. Haleiwa Beach is a narrow, palm-fringed beach, bordered by coral. It is, however, a good place for swimming, fishing and surfing. The park also has baseball and basketball facilities, and showers and restrooms.

Well worth visiting, too, and also located on Kamehameha Highway (83), near the corner of Emerson Road, is the Liliuokalani Church, originally built in 1832, and featuring a steeple and walls of coral and wood. The church has in it, of interest to visitors, a unique, 100-year-old clock that shows not only the time, day of the week and month, but also the phase of the moon. The church is of course named for Queen Liliuokalani, Hawaii's last monarch, who succeeded her brother, King Kalakaua.

Northeastward from Haleiwa, of course, lies the North Shore, but a short detour westward, a mile or so, will take you to Waialua, another sleepy little plantation town, with a sugar mill and a school, and which, in turn, has to the west of it, another 4½ miles distant, the Mokuleia Beach Park, located just off Farrington Highway (930), and well worth visiting. Mokuleia is a 12-acre beach park, with a long, narrow beach, bordered by some coral and backed by shallow dunes. There is also a large grassy area at the park, with showers and restrooms, and picnic tables and some camping possibilities. The beach, however, attracts primarily windsurfers and fishermen, as swimming is not encouraged here due to the adverse ocean conditions.

A mile west of Mokuleia beach, on the *mauka*—inland—side of the highway (930), lies Dillingham Airfield, used by small plane and glider tour companies, and named for pioneer land baron Benjamin Dillingham, founder of the Oahu Railway & Land Company which operated a railroad from Kaena to Haleiwa during the early 1900s; and another two miles west of there, Farrington Highway (930) ends, with the shoreline continuing another five miles or so to Kaena Point, the westernmost point on the island.

In any case, let us now return to Haleiwa and the North Shore, and our main route of travel, Kamehameha Highway (83). Here, northeastward along the highway, some 2 miles from Haleiwa lies the Kawailoa Beach, which is itself made up of two distinct beach sections, Laniakea and Chun's Reef, both popular surfing spots. Laniakea, of course, is the first of the two beaches, quite long, and bordered by a coral reef just offshore, and with Chun's Reef lying just to the northeast of it, another half mile distant. Both beaches feature spectacular, outsized waves in the winter months. There are, however, no facilities at these beaches, and swimming is not encouraged, due to the the strong ocean currents here.

From Chun's Reef, it is another one and three-quarter miles to the Waimea Bay Beach Park, with its beautiful, crescent-shaped beach spilling over into a picture-perfect aquamarine bay. This is of course one of the most popular beach parks on the North Shore, and the site of several surf contests each year, including the prestigious Quicksilver/Eddie Aikau Memorial Big Wave Classic which is held only in

Oahu

certain conditions—when the waves crest at over 20 feet! There is also, as an added attraction, a large, rocky outcropping on the southeast side of the bay, known as the "Rock," from where thrill-seekers can frequently be seen plunging into the ocean. In any event, facilities at the beach park include a lifeguard, picnic tables, showers and restrooms; swimming, however, is not advisable during the winter months due the overwhelming surf.

Directly across from Waimea Bay Beach Park, on the *mauka*— inland—side of the highway (83), the Waimea Falls Park fans out into the ancient, 1,800-acre Waimea Valley—one of the most sacred valleys on the island, where the Hawaiian religion once flourished. Waimea Falls Park, however, is now one of the most popular visitor attractions on the North Shore, which has in it not only several historical sites— including remnants of *heiaus* and a fishing shrine, archaeological sites, and a series of age-old stone platforms—but also a botanical garden where you can see nearly 6,000 species of tropical flora from around the world, including more than 400 species of rare and endangered Hawaiian and South Pacific plants, all labeled for easy identification. There are narrated tram tours as well as guided walks of the park, and several colorful events to interest the visitor, such as cliff diving at the 45-foot-high Waimea Falls, *hula* performances, and an assortment of traditional Hawaiian sports and games, among them *o'o ihe*, the ancient sport of spear throwing. There are also some good swimming possibilities in the natural pool at the foot of the falls, and hiking trails winding through the heart of the Waimea Valley. Besides which, there are a restaurant, snack bar and gift shops on the premises as well. The park is open to the public daily.

Try to also visit the St. Peter and Paul Mission, also located off Kamehameha Highway, across from the Waimea Bay Beach Park, just to the northeast of mile marker 6. Interestingly, the church was once part of a rock-crushing plant, and transformed into a church in 1953. The church and its tower can be easily seen from Waimea Bay, quite distinctive in its architecture.

Also of interest, northeastward from Waimea Bay Beach Park, about a mile, lies the Pupukea Beach Park, comprised of two areas of interest: the Three Tables, which is in fact a small, sandy beach, sur-rounded by lava, tidepools and a coral reef, and named for the three lava ledges seen rising from the water just offshore; and Shark's Cove, an essentially rocky shoreline area with tidepools. Both Shark's Cove and the Three Tables offer good snorkeling and diving possibilities in the summer months, and also camping facilities, basketball courts, children's play areas, and showers and restrooms.

East from Pupukea Beach, of course, a half mile on Pupukea Road—which goes off Kamehameha Highway—there is yet another place of supreme interest, the Pu'uomahuka Heiau State Monument. The Pu'uomahuka Heiau, meaning "Hill of Escape," is in fact the largest *heiau* on Oahu, 575 feet long and 170 feet wide, believed to have been built by the legendary *menehune*, Hawaii's mysterious little people who are credited with scores of other architectural marvels around the islands. The *heiau* itself, situated at an elevation of approx-imately 300 feet, overlooking Waimea Bay and the North Shore, comprises three large terraces, each defined by a low stone wall along its perimeter. There is also a paved trail that journeys around the *heiau*, open to visitors. Interestingly, the Pu'uomahuka Heiau was also a sacred place for Hawaiian royalty, where royal babies were given birth, and, too, the site of human sacrifices, where in 1794 three of British sea captain George Vancouver's crew were sacrificed.

Farther still, some one and one-half miles northeast of Pupukea Beach Park, located along the Kamehameha Highway (83), is Ehukai Beach Park, home to the spectacular "Banzai Pipeline"—the most famous wave in Hawaii, with a 200-yard break, and an almost-perfect tube, rising to heights of 20 to 30 feet. This, needless to say, is also the site of several surfing competitions in the winter months each year, and a good place to watch world-class surfers in action. Besides which, the beach itself, long, wide, and bordered by ironwood trees, has good facilities, including a lifeguard, picnic tables, and showers and restrooms.

Northeast of Ehukai Beach, three-quarters of a mile along the highway (83), lies the Sunset Beach Park, another premier surfing spot, where, again, you can watch some the world's best surfers compete for coveted prizes, riding waves that, in the winter months, can often rise as high as 30 feet. The beach, in any case, is a long, palm-fringed white-sand beach, bordered by a coral reef just offshore, and with an on-duty lifeguard, and portable toilets. There is also, by the way, a section of the beach along the east side, just off Sunset Point, known as "Backdoors," where windsurfers can be seen honing their skills.

Finally, there is Turtle Bay, some 4 miles from Sunset Beach, which has at its northeast end, at Kuilima Point, the Turtle Bay Hilton and Country Club—a 486-room luxury hotel with an 18-hole championship golf course, the Arnold Palmer Championship Golf Course. The Turtle Bay Hilton is of course the North Shore's only resort hotel, originally built in 1972 by casino owner Del Webb, and refurbished and upgraded in 1983 by the Hilton corporation, at an estimated cost of $17 million. The resort now boasts, besides its golf course, tennis courts, horseback riding and dune cycling facilities for its guests, and two first class restaurants. There is, in addition, a lovely, small, sandy beach here, along Kuilima Cove, situated between two lava outcroppings, and with abundant coral and a protective reef just offshore, making it an especially good place for snorkeling and swimming in calm weather. There are showers and restrooms at the beach, and also some kayak rentals.

WINDWARD COAST

The Windward Coast of Oahu is rather lovely, largely unspoiled and remarkably picturesque, with the lofty Ko'olau cliffs to the west, frequently overhung by low clouds and coastal mist, and giving way, to the east, to lush valleys and windswept plains, and, beyond, the open ocean. The coast itself—named for the frequently fierce trade winds that gather strength as they blow inland from the ocean, toward the Ko'olau range—stretches some 30 miles, northwest-southeast, from Kahuku at its top end to Kaneohe and Kailua—the principal towns here—and southeastward another 8 miles or so to Waimanalo and Makapu'u Point, the easternmost point on the island.

Kahuku to Kailua

It is, of course, possible to explore the Windward Coast either north to south or south to north. However, for the purposes of our tour, since we are already on the North Shore, let us begin at the northern end, at Kahuku Point, a little finger of land jutting out directly northward at the northeastern tip of the island, which has the distinction of being the northernmost point on the Windward Coast and, too, on the island. There are, needless to say, superb, all-round ocean views to be enjoyed from here.

Just to the southeast of Kahuku Point, 3 miles or so on the Kamehameha Highway (83), lies a town of the same name, Kahuku. Kahuku is a sleepy little former plantation town, where you can still visit the old sugar mill building, dating from 1890 and now housing the Kahuku Sugar Mill Shopping Center, with a handful of shops and a restaurant. There are also self-guided tours of the mill, on which you can view some of the old mill machinery, including the original steam engine, its outsized gears and crankshaft, primary crusher, and smasher, all painted in bright colors, and with good descriptions of each part. The mill-cum-shopping center is open to the public daily, 10 a.m. to 5 p.m.

Journeying southward, a little over a mile from Kahuku, on the *makai*—ocean—side of the highway, is the Malaekahana Bay State Recreation Area, situated at the head of Malaekahana Bay, and quite popular with island families. The bay is of course described by two points, Makahoa Point and Kalanai Point, to its north and south, respectively, with a small island, Moku Auia—also known as Goat Island—located just offshore from Kalanai Point. There is also a beach here, long, narrow, and curving along the bay, bordered by clusters of coral and lined, to its back, by ironwood and hala trees. Malaekahana Bay, besides, has good swimming and camping possibilities, and picnic tables, barbecue pits, showers and restrooms.

A mile south of Malaekahana Bay lies Laie, a village, no more, but which has in it two places of interest: the Hawaii Mormon Temple

56 Oahu

WINDWARD COAST

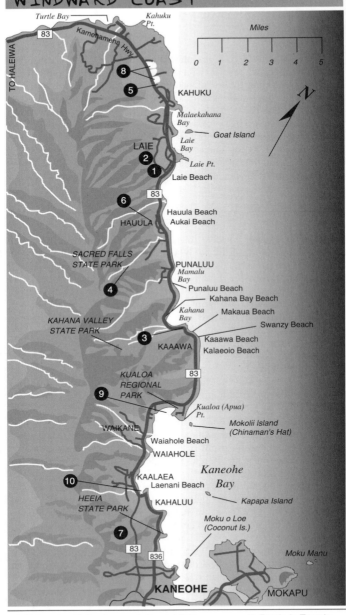

1. Polynesian Cultural Center
2. Mormon Temple
3. Crouching Lion
4. Sacred Falls
5. Kahuku Sugar Mill
6. Lanakila Church
7. Byodo-In Temple
8. Aquaculture Farms
9. Molii Fishpond
10. Kahaluu Fishpond

and the Polynesian Cultural Center. The first of these, situated on Hale La'a Boulevard—which goes off the highway (83) westward, just to the north of Laie—is a replica of the Mormon Temple in Salt Lake City. It was built in 1919, from volcanic rock and concrete, at a cost of around $200,000, and is set on manicured grounds dotted with palms and a series of pools. There is also a visitors center at the church, with films and information on the church, and highlights of the history of the Mormon missionaries in Hawaii, who first arrived in Oahu in 1860.

The Polynesian Cultural Center, located on Kamehameha Highway, south from the Hawaii Temple, is undoubtedly the greater attraction. It is in fact the second most visited sight on the island—after the USS Arizona Memorial at Pearl Harbor—drawing nearly a million tourists each year. The center, established in 1963 by The Church of Jesus Christ of Latter Day Saints, actually comprises some 42 acres, featuring seven recreated Polynesian villages, highlighting the cultures of the South Pacific, representing Samoa, New Zealand, Tahiti, Fiji, the Marquesas, Tonga and old Hawaii. At each of the villages, the Polynesian people demonstrate their arts and craft and way of life, including *poi* pounding, making tapa cloth from tree bark, and coconut husking. There are also walking tours of the facility, as well as canoe trips through lagoons that connect the villages. The greatest lures at the center, however, are its lavish buffet and luau dinner shows, notable among them the afternoon "Pageant of the Long Canoes," a floating parade of Polynesian song and dance, and "This is Polynesia," another South Pacific song and dance extravaganza, featured in the evenings.

Also at Laie, you can visit Laie Point, reached by way of Anemoku Street—which goes off Kamehameha Highway (83), a half-mile or so north of the Polynesian Cultural Center—then east—right—on Naupaka Street, and right again on the Laie Point road a little way to Laie Point. Laie Point is a remarkable vista point, overlooking a natural sea arch directly offshore, and Goat Island to the north and the Windward Coast to the south.

In any event, southeastward from Laie, roughly a half mile, is Pounder's Beach, a crescent-shaped beach, backed by a grassy area and *hala* and ironwood trees, and quite popular with bodysurfers; and another mile to the south, at the little village of Hau'ula, is the Hau'ula Beach Park, a long, narrow roadside beach, bordered by a coral reef and backed by ironwood and palm trees, with good swimming and snorkeling possibilities. Also of interest, directly west—inland—from Hau'ula Beach are the stone ruins of a congregational church, the Lanakila Church, built here in 1853, and partly dismantled and removed from here a few years later, in 1897.

Southward, another half mile, is the entrance to the idyllic Sacred Falls State Park, a 1,374-acre nature preserve with an 80-foot-high waterfall—the Sacred Falls, or, in Hawaiian, the Kaliuwa'a Falls. The waterfall is located deep inside the park, reached by way of a frequently-slippery 2-mile foot trail that leads from the parking area near the park entrance, passing through some lush vegetation, to the falls. At the foot of the falls, of course, there is a natural pool—bottomless, we are told, in which lives a demon, restrained by the sheer force of the falling water. The pool, in any case, is ideal for swimming or splashing around in.

Farther still, southeastward along the Kamehameha Highway, some 2 miles from the Sacred Falls park entrance, is the Punalu'u Beach Park, a long, narrow roadside beach, bordered by rocks and a coral reef, and, to its back, by ironwood trees. The beach has good swimming and snorkeling possibilities, due to the protective reef just offshore. There are also picnic tables here, and showers and restroom facilities.

Another 2 miles or so and we are at Kahana Bay, described by Makali'i Point and Mahie Point, and the Kahana Bay Beach Park, an 8-acre park with a beautiful, crescent-shaped white-sand beach, backed by ironwood trees. The Kahana Bay beach, needless to say, offers good, safe swimming conditions, and also picnic tables, restrooms, and a boat-launching ramp at its north end. There are also some fishing possibilities here, and views, looking southeastward, of the ancient Huila Pond, located a half mile or so distant, and built, according to popular belief, by the *menehune*, Hawaii's legendary pixie-like people who worked only at night.

Directly across from the Kahana Bay Beach Park, on the *mauka* —inland—side of the highway (83), lies the Kahana Valley State Park, comprising an ancient, 5,267-acre valley, where, it is believed, the first Polynesians to arrive in Hawaii originally settled. The valley is now preserved as a "living park," with its residents educating visitors in Hawaiian culture and way of life.

Yet another place of interest here, just to the east of Kahana Bay, roughly a half mile, on the *mauka*—inland—side of the highway, is the Crouching Lion Inn, formerly the home of a construction engineer, built in 1928; and directly behind the inn rises the mountain known as Kauhi'imakaokalani, or "Crouching Lion"—part of the Ko'olau Range —which, in form, vaguely resembles a crouching lion. According to a popular myth, it was here, along this mountain ridge, that Kauhi'ima-kaokalani, a demigod and the "watchtower of heaven," arrived from Tahiti with Pele, the goddess of fire, and was subsequently turned to stone. Kauhi then asked Pele's sister, Hi'iaka, to be set free, but was firmly turned down. This, in turn, angered Kauhi, and he tried to raise himself from the mountain ridge, but his strength, or the lack thereof, only enabled him to realign himself into a crouching position, where he has remained since.

In any event, southeast from the Crouching Lion, another half mile, is the Swanzy Beach Park, a multi-use shoreline park, situated just off the highway, with baseball and basketball facilities, swings, picnic tables, restrooms and showers; and just to the south of there lies the sleepy little town of Ka'a'awa, which has in it the Ka'a'awa Beach Park, a small, narrow roadside beach with a protective coral reef, offering good, safe swimming and snorkeling more or less year-round.

Also at Ka'a'awa, a little to the south of Ka'a'awa Beach Park, is the Kalaeolio Beach Park, located alongside the highway (83), with the Ka'a'awa Stream just to the south of it. Kalaeolio is a small beach,

Oahu 59

backed by ironwood trees, and with generally good swimming and snorkeling conditions.

Another beach here, situated roughly a mile south of Kalaeolio Beach, is the Kanenelu Beach, a long, narrow roadside beach, frequented primarily by fishermen, surfers, beachcombers, and dedicated swimmers. The beach, however, is largely undeveloped, with no facilities for visitors.

From Kanenelu Beach, a mile or so south along the highway (83) lie the ruins of the Kualoa Sugar Mill, originally built here in 1863, and which remained in operation until 1871; and a half mile south of there, also of interest, is the 150-acre Kualoa Regional Park, once one of the most sacred places on Oahu, where newborn *ali'i*—noblemen—were instructed in the art of warfare and the customs and traditions of Hawaiian chiefs, and where, also, breakers of *kapu* sought refuge. The park, in any case, has a narrow beach, bordered by coral, and a large, grassy area dotted with palm trees. Beach facilities include a lifeguard, picnic tables, showers and restrooms. The beach also offers good, and generally safe, swimming conditions.

Nearby, too, on the southwest side of the Kualoa Regional Park is the Moli'i Fishpond, a 124-acre fishpond with a 4,000-foot enclosing wall, believed to have been built by the *menehune*, Hawaii's mysterious little people; and just offshore from the park, looking eastward, you can see Mokoli'i Island, also known as "Chinaman's Hat," named for its distinctive shape. Legend endures that the Hawaiian goddess of fire Pele's sister, Hi'iaka, was once walking along on a nearby trail, when she was confronted by a fierce dragon. Hi'iaka, needless to say, slew the dragon, and its tail she tossed into the ocean—just offshore from here—the tip of which can still be seen, just above the water.

South from Kauloa Regional Park, some 2 to 3 miles, lie the tiny communities of Waikane and Waiahole, situated in lush, green surroundings, and dotted with roadside fruit stands. This is of course a rather fertile area, where, in the early days, *taro* was grown in vast quantities, in terraced fields. A contemporary Hawaiian song, "Sweet Lady of Waiahole," romanticizes old Waiahole, with the story of a Hawaiian woman beginning each day with the gathering of sweet island fruit here, then setting off down the road to sell it at the roadside.

In any event, some 2 miles or so south from Waiahole, on the *makai*—ocean—side of the highway, you can search out the ancient Kahalu'u Fishpond, with its 1,200-foot-long enclosing wall; and directly southeast from there, another 3 miles, approximately, on the coastal Kamehameha Highway—which now becomes highway 836—lies He'eia State Park, a largely grassy area with shade trees. The park, situated on Kealohi Point, overlooks Kaneohe Bay and, to the south, the He'eia Fishpond—an ancient, 88-acre fishpond, with a 5,000-foot-long enclosing wall, which once also featured 4 watch-houses to watch the fish movements. There are also good views from here, looking southeastward, of Moku o Loe, also known as Coconut Island.

Just south of the Kahalu'u Fishpond too—2 miles south of Waiahole—Kahekili Highway (83) branches off Kamehameha Highway (836) and heads off directly southward, inland, but parallel to the coastal Kamehameha Highway; and 2 miles or so along the Kahekili Highway, we enter the Valley of the Temples, in which stands the glorious Byodo-In Temple, a splendid replica of a 900-year-old Buddhist temple in Kyoto, Japan. The Byodo-In Temple, built in 1968, nearly 100 years after the arrival of the first Japanese in Hawaii, enjoys a dramatic setting at the foot of the emerald, more or less vertical Ko'olau *pali*—cliffs—that rise in spires directly behind the temple, frequently overhung by coastal mist. There is a large, 3-ton ceremonial brass bell at the temple, and also, seated on a carved lotus in the main temple building, a 9-foot gold-and-lacquer Buddha. The temple is of course surrounded by delightful, landscaped Japanese gardens, which also feature a 2-acre reflecting pond, stocked with swans, ducks, and thousands of carp—a symbol of eternity, order and perseverance. There are, besides, a Tea House—which serves refreshments—and a gift shop on the premises.

In any case, it is approximately one and one-half miles south from either the Byodo-In Temple on Kahekili Highway (83) or the He'eia State Park on Kamehameha Highway (836), to the sprawling coastal community of Kaneohe, situated at the head of Kaneohe Bay. At Kaneohe, which is largely urbanized, the only place of interest is the Ho'omaluhia Botanical Garden, located at the end of Luluku Road, which goes off Kamehameha Highway, just south of Likelike Highway (63). The lush, 400-acre gardens feature plants and trees from various parts of the world, including the Philippines, Malaysia, the Americas, Africa, Australia, India, Sri Lanka and Hawaii. There are several hiking and horseback riding trails here as well, and a 32-acre lake where, unfortunately, swimming is not permitted. There is also a visitor center at the gardens, with maps and information for garden tours and other scheduled programs. The gardens are open to the public daily.

Adjacent to Kaneohe, to the east, lies Kailua, another suburban community, which, nevertheless, has as its chief attraction Kailua Beach, one of the loveliest white-sand beaches on Oahu. The beach—accessed on Kailua Road, which goes off the Pali Highway (61)—is long and wide, with a gently-sloping sandy bottom and crystal-clear aquamarine water, offering good, and generally safe, swimming conditions year-round, making it especially attractive to children. Kailua Beach also, we might add, is notable as the birthplace of windsurfing, where, in 1975, the pioneering Naish family first developed the sport, combining surfing and sailing. Needless to say, windsurfing continues to be popular here.

Try to also visit Lanikai Beach, another beautiful white-sand beach, situated just to the south of Kailua Beach, and accessed from Mokulua Drive, which goes off the one-way A'alapapa Drive. Lanikai Beach is nearly a mile long, lined with beachfront homes, and, due to a lack of facilities, less crowded than Kailua Beach. Lanikai, however, not unlike Kailua Beach, also offers good, and generally safe, swimming conditions year-round.

Another place of interest, located inland from the Kailua and Lanikai beaches, is the Ulupo Heiau State Historical Site, reached by way of Pali Highway (61) east from the intersection of Kalanianaole Highway (72) a short distance, then north on Ulupo Street a block or

Oahu   61

so, and right—east—onto Manu Aloha Street, and, again, right—or south—on Manu O'o Street which leads directly to the YMCA, from where a leisurely walk eastward will take you to the *heiau*. The Ulupo Heiau, 180 feet long and 140 feet wide, is believed to have been built by the *menehune*, Hawaii's industrious—and mysterious—little people, who worked only at night, completing entire projects in the course of a single night. Ulupo, interestingly, means "night inspiration," a tribute, no doubt, to the *menehune*. The *heiau* site also has good views of the Kawainui Swamp, just to the west.

Southeast to Waimanalo

From Kailua, you can follow Kalanianaole Highway (72) southeastward, some 3 or 4 miles, to Waimanalo, a small town at the southern end of the Ko'olau Range, and Waimanalo Beach, an adjoining beach community, situated at the head of Waimanalo Bay. The chief interest here, of course, lies in the beaches, which make up, more or less, the entire shoreline along the bay. There are, in fact, five well-liked beaches here, strung along Waimanalo Bay, northernmost among them the Bellows Field Beach Park, a 46-acre park with a long, sandy beach, located approximately a mile northwest of Waimanalo, at the Bellows Air Force Station, just off Kalanianaole Highway. The beach is quite popular with vacationing families, and surfers and fishermen. It offers good, safe swimming conditions, and camping on the weekends.

Just to the southeast of Bellows Field Beach Park, a mile or so the highway (72), lies the Waimanalo Bay State Recreation Area, with its long, white-sand beach, backed by a thicket of ironwood trees, popularly known as "Sherwood Forest," for its notoriety during the 1960s, as a haven for petty thieves. The beach park, nevertheless, is now quite popular with surfers and bodysurfers, and it has, besides, some picnic tables for park visitors, and showers and restrooms.

Directly south of the Waimanalo Bay State Recreation Area, also off Kalanianaole Highway (72), is the Waimanalo Beach Park, an increasingly popular, long white-sand beach, curving around Waimanalo Bay, backed by shallow sand dunes and ironwood trees. The beach park has a baseball field, basketball courts, picnic tables, showers and restroom facilities. It also has good swimming and camping possibilities.

Southeastward from Waimanalo Beach on the Kalanianaole Highway, a little way, lies the Kaiona Beach Park, a narrow, rocky beach, protected by an outer reef and backed by a grassy area; and southeast from there, another one and one-half miles, is Kaupo Beach, a small, sandy beach, bordered by clusters of coral, and frequented, primarily, by surfers and fishermen.

From Kaupo Beach, it is approximately a mile on the highway (72) to Makapu'u Point, the easternmost point on the island, southwest of which lies East Honolulu.

WAIANAE COAST

The Waianae Coast—or the leeward coast—stretches north-westward from Ewa Beach—which lies just to the west of Honolulu, some 7 or 8 miles—to Nanakuli, Waianae, Makaha and Kaena Point, the westernmost point on the island. It is of course an area that is primarily dry and arid, but which, nevertheless, unfurls inland into beautiful, deep valleys, backed by the lofty Waianae Range which has as its highest point Mount Ka'ala, with an elevation of 4,020 feet — the highest point on the island. The Waianae Coast, however, it must be fair to say, is a marginal side of Oahu, largely undeveloped, often unfriendly, remote, and attracting, for the most part, visitors with a penchant for adventure and exploring off the beaten path.

In any case, the Waianae Coast can be accessed from Honolulu by way of the all-important freeway, H1, westward to Pearl City and Waipahu, then directly west toward the coast, where it merges with the Farrington Highway (93)—the main route of travel along the Waianae Coast. But before reaching the coast, a short detour south on Fort Weaver Road—which goes off the freeway, H1, just to the west of Waipahu—leads to Ewa (3 miles), an old plantation town, lost in time, and Ewa Beach (5 miles) which has two beach parks of interest —Oneula and Ewa. The Ewa Beach Park, in particular, is well worth investigating, for it has a large, sandy beach, bordered by a coral reef, and with good views of Honolulu and Diamond Head. There is also a large grassy area here, and a baseball facility, basketball court, children's play area, picnic tables, and showers and restrooms.

Another detour, some 5 miles west of Waipahu on the freeway (H1), then south on Kalaeloa Boulevard and southwest on Olai Street a short distance, is Barbers Point Beach Park—a narrow, coral-lined beach, where there are some picnic tables and restroom facilities, and which also has views, looking eastward, of Diamond Head. The beach, interestingly, is named for an English sea captain, Henry Barber, who ran aground here in 1796, and later became a friend to Kamehameha I.

Westward from the Barbers Point detour, however, just past the intersection of Kalaeloa Boulevard, the highway, H1, becomes the Farrington Highway (93), and leads another 3 miles or so north-westward to Kahe Point, located at the south end of the Waianae Coast. Here, just to the north of Kahe Point, is the Kahe Point Beach Park, situated on low cliffs and bordered by coral and rocks, frequented primarily by fishermen; and another quarter mile to the north of there lies Manners Beach, a small strand of golden sand, backed by *kiawe* trees and sand dunes, and quite attractive to surfers and beachcombers.

North from Kahe Point and Manners Beach, roughly a mile, lies Nanakuli, a small town with a few shops, which also has its very own beach, the Nanakuli Beach Park. Nanakuli Beach, in fact, comprises two crescent-shaped coves with golden sand, separated by low cliffs and coral. There are good swimming and snorkeling possibilities here in summer, when the ocean is relatively calm; however, swimming is

Oahu 63

WAIANAE COAST

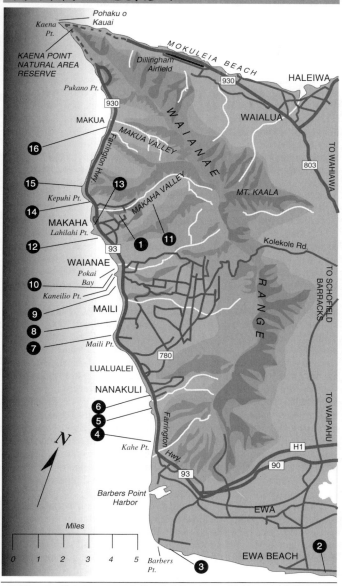

1. Sheraton Makaha Resort
2. Ewa Beach
3. Barbers Point Beach
4. Kahe Point Beach
5. Manners Beach
6. Nanakuli Beach
7. Ulehawa Beach
8. Maili Beach
9. Lualualei Beach
10. Pokai Bay Beach
11. Kaneaki Heiau
12. Maunalahilahi Beach
13. Papaoneone Beach
14. Makaha Beach
15. Kepuhi Beach
16. Makua Beach

not advised during the winter months due to the adverse ocean conditions. The beach also has lifeguard stations, picnic tables, camping facilities, showers and restrooms. Besides which, there is a local community center located here, as well as a children's play area and a ball field.

Northwestward from Nanakuli, another mile or so, and we are at the Ulehawa Beach Park #1, strung alongside the highway. Ulehawa is a long, narrow, sandy beach, alongside which the Ulehawa Stream drains into the ocean. The beach is bordered by a coral reef, with a few sandy areas, and backed by shallow sand dunes, lined with palm trees and *kiawe*. Swimming, however, is not advised here, due to the dangerous ocean conditions.

Another beach, the Ulehawa Beach Park #2, lies some 2 miles farther along the coast, just to the north of Maili Point. The Ulehawa Beach Park #2, again, is one of the less attractive beaches, sandy, but interspersed with abundant coral. There are some surfing possibilities here, although swimming is not advised during the winter months. The beach has a restroom, and some picnic tables.

Also of interest, adjoining to the north of Maili Point and Ulehawa Beach Park #2, is Maili Beach Park, which extends a mile and comprises, for the most part, pockets of sand and coral, and a large, grassy area with picnic tables, swings and a jungle gym. The beach has a lifeguard station at its north end, and showers and restrooms. There are also some swimming possibilities during the summer months and in calm seas, and surfing in the winter months.

North still, another mile along the highway (93), lies Waianae, another small town, with a shopping center, and which has, just to its south, the Lualualei Beach Park. Lualualei is a long beach, randomly punctuated with coral, but which, in all fairness, is one of the less attractive beaches, frequently overrun by groups of derelicts and unfriendly natives. The beach, nevertheless, has some restroom facilities.

At Waianae, too, just north of the Lualualei Beach, is the Pokai Bay Beach, situated at the south end of the small Pokai Bay, on the *makai*—ocean—side of Farrington Highway (93), directly across from the intersection of the Waianae Valley Road. Pokai Bay Beach is one of the more hospitable beaches on the Waianae Coast, crescent shaped, sandy, and protected by breakwaters from the open ocean, thus offering some of the safest swimming conditions on the leeward side of the island. There is a large, grassy area here as well, and picnic tables, an on-duty lifeguard, showers and restrooms.

Of interest, too, at the southwest end of Pokai Bay Beach, at Kane'ilio Point, is the historic Kuilioloa Heiau, unique in that it is surrounded on three sides by water. The *heiau* itself is 150 feet long and 35 feet wide, and features three platforms, all descending to Kane'ilio Point. Kuilioloa, interestingly, named for an ancient Hawaiian dog that is well remembered for protecting travelers, was once a place of refuge for travelers. It is also believed to have provided Kamehameha I and his warriors a resting place, while on their way to invade Kauai.

Northwest from Waianae, however, some 2 miles on Farrington Highway, lies Makaha, the westernmost town on the island. Makaha has one or two shops, and three sandy beaches—Mauna Lahilahi, Papaoneone and Makaha Beach. Mauna Lahilahi is of course the southernmost, located directly across from the intersection of the highway (93) and Makaha Valley Road. It is essentially a roadside beach, bordered by coral, which has some picnic tables for visitors, and showers and restroom facilities. Swimming, however, is not encouraged here during the winter months, primarily due to the ocean swells and strong undercurrents.

Papaoneone Beach is situated another half mile from Mauna Lahilahi, northwestward, alongside the highway, with a small access road dashing off between Lahilahi and Moua roads. Papaoneone features a lovely cove, and a quarter-mile-long beach, with some swimming as well as surfing possibilities, although caution is advised, especially in the winter months.

Makaha, the northernmost beach at the Makaha township, is located another one and one-quarter miles northwest of Papaoneone Beach, alongside Farrington Highway. Makaha is a large, golden-sand beach, bordered by some clusters of coral. It is also a very popular surfing spot, with winter waves reaching heights of nearly 30 feet, and the site of several surfing contests, notable among them Buffalo's Big Board Surfing Classic, held in February each year. The beach also has some good swimming possibilities in the summer months, and showers, restrooms, and an on-duty lifeguard.

At Makaha, too, on Makaha Valley Road, is the former Sheraton Makaha hotel, now closed as a resort, but which still has an 18-hole, championship golf course, the West Course, open to the public, and with the distinction of being one of the longest courses in the islands, at 7,093 yards.

Also at Makaha, well worth investigating, is the Kaneaki Heiau, reached by way of Makaha Valley Road—which goes off the highway northeastward, directly across from Lahilahi Beach—some one and three-quarter miles, then Maunaolu Street, a private road, to the right —or east—another half mile, to Alahele Street, which leads to the *heiau* parking area. The Kaneaki Heiau, in any case, is one of the best preserved *heiaus* on Oahu, situated in the lush Makaha Valley, amid *ti* plants and groves of palm, guava and banana trees. The *heiau*, built between 1470 and 1640, and modified and enlarged no fewer than three times, is 150 feet long and 75 feet wide, comprising an altar surrounded by *tikis*—or idols—and two thatched houses—Halemana, which is the "house of spiritual power," and Halepahu, the "drum house." The *heiau*, it is believed, was originally built as temple for the worship of good harvest, but was converted, during its third modification, into a war temple, where, between 1795 and 1810, Kamehameha I prepared his warriors for battle with the kingdom of Kauai.

Northwestward still, 2 or 3 miles from Makaha, along Farrington Highway (93), lies Kea'au Beach Park, a shoreline park with a large, grassy area with picnic tables under *kiawe* trees. There are also some camping possibilities here, and showers and restrooms. However, we must point out that there is no beach as such at Kea'au, and swimming, too, is not advised due to the unfavorable ocean conditions.

Farther, a little way, some one and one-half miles from Kea'au Beach, on the *mauka*—inland—side of the highway (93), you can search out the Kaneana Cave, approximately 100 feet deep and 40 feet wide. Kaneana, which, in Hawaiian, means "Cave of God," was once a sacred place, the site of several ancient Hawaiian ceremonies, and also, we are told, the home of a shark goddess and of demigod Maui and his grandmother. Sadly, though, the cave is now largely neglected, and defaced with graffiti.

Yet another beach, the Makua Beach, is located roughly 3 miles north of Makaha, reached directly on the main highway (93). Makua is a broad, sandy beach, which, in ancient times, provided a canoe landing for travelers. The beach, however, more recently, has become somewhat less attractive—not unlike some of the other beaches on the leeward coast—primarily due to the growing presence of long-term campers. There are no facilities here.

Finally, there is the Kaena Point Natural Area Reserve, situated at the end of Farrington Highway, some five and one-half miles northwest of Makaha, and with a long, golden-sand beach, backed by shallow sand dunes. There are good views from here, westward, of Kaena Point, the westernmost point on the island. There is also a 2-mile trail that journeys along a flat, arid stretch, from the reserve to the end of the island, at Kaena Point. Of interest, too, just offshore from Kaena Point, is Pohaku O Kauai, a huge boulder that, according to local lore, settled here when Hawaiian demigod Maui, in his attempt to unite the islands of Oahu and Kauai—some 95 miles to the northwest—cast and sank his magnificent hook, Manaiakalani, into the base of the island of Kauai, then tugged on the line with all his might, only to break off a piece of the island—the boulder, Pohaku O Kauai—which landed here, at his feet.

Oahu 67

PRACTICAL INFORMATION FOR OAHU

HOW TO GET THERE

Oahu is situated approximately 25 miles northwest of Molokai, or 75 miles northwest of Maui, with the island of Kauai farther to its northwest, some 95 miles distant. From San Francisco, the island is 2,360 miles distant; from Los Angeles, 2,550 miles; and from Tokyo, 3,830 miles. It can be reached directly from the U.S. mainland, as well as several international cities, on scheduled flights on any of more than a dozen different domestic and international airlines. Oahu's principal airport, the Honolulu International Airport, is located in Honolulu, near the southwestern end of the city.

Direct to Honolulu

Domestic Airlines. The following domestic airlines service the Honolulu Airport: *American Airlines*, (800) 433-7300; *Continental Airlines*, (800) 523-3273; *Delta Airlines*, (800) 221-1212; *Hawaiian Airlines*, (800) 822-8811; *Northwest Airlines*, (800) 225-2525; and *United Airlines*, (800) 241-6522.

International Airlines. The following international airlines offer scheduled flights to Honolulu: *American Airlines*, (800) 433-7300; *Air New Zealand*, (800) 252-1234; *Canadian Airlines International*, (800) 426-7000; *China Airlines*, (808) 955-0088; *Continental Airlines*, (800) 231-0856; *Delta Airlines*, (800) 221-1212; *Hawaiian Airlines*, (800) 882-8811; *Japan Air Lines*, (800) 232-2517; *Korea Air*, (808) 923-7302; *Northwest Airlines*, (800) 225-2525; *Philippine Airlines*, (800) 435-9725; *Qantas Airways*, (800) 227-4500; *Singapore Airlines*, (808) 542-6063; and *United Airlines*, (800) 241-6522.

Inter-island Flights

Flights are also available between Oahu and the other Hawaiian islands, Maui, Kauai, Hawaii, Molokai and Lanai. The following airlines offer regular, scheduled inter-island flights between Honolulu, Oahu, and the other islands: *Air Molokai*, (808) 877-0026; *Aloha Airlines*, (808) 244-9071; *Aloha Island Air*, (800) 652-6541; and *Hawaiian Airlines*, (800) 882-8811. Fares, typically, range from $49-$99 one-way, to $98-$138 round-trip.

TOURIST INFORMATION

Hawaii Visitors Bureau (HVB) - Oahu. *HVB Main Office,* Waikiki Business Plaza, 2250 Kalakaua Ave., Suite 514, Honolulu, HI 96815; (808) 923-1811. Wealth of tourist information available, including directory of accommodations and restaurants and a calendar of events. Also maps, and a tourist publication, *The Island of Hawaii: A Vacation Planner,* covering places of interest on the islands, recreation and tours. The *Hawaii Visitors Bureau* maintains offices at the following locations: *HVB Los Angeles,* 3440 Wilshire Blvd., Suite 502, Los Angeles, CA 90010, (213) 385-5301; *HVB San Francisco,* 50 California St., Suite 450, San Francisco, CA 94111, (415) 392-8173.

Waikiki Oahu Visitors Association. 1001 Bishop St., Suite 880; (808) 524-0722.

Hawaii Chamber of Commerce. 735 Bishop St., Suite 220, Honolulu, HI 96815; (808) 545-4300. Visitor information brochures, including lodging, restaurant and tour company listings.

Publications. There are also several free publications available on the island, at airports, hotels, restaurants and shopping centers, with valuable tourist information and articles of local interest. The following are among the best-known—the *Drive Guide*, published three times a year and available at rental car agencies, offers information on dining, island activities and sightseeing, and includes maps; *Guide to Oahu*, published monthly, contains information on dining and entertainment, shopping, island activities and sightseeing, as well as maps and coupons; *Spotlight Oahu,* a monthly magazine, offers tips on dining, shopping, fun activities and sightseeing, with maps and coupons; *This Week Oahu,* a weekly magazine, contains information on activities on the island, and shopping, dining and sightseeing, as well as maps and discount coupons; and *Waikiki Beach Press,* published weekly on Mondays, features up-to-date information on dining, entertainment, activities and island adventures, and also contains island maps and discount coupons.

HOW TO GET AROUND

By Car. Rental cars are available from several different car rental agencies on the island. Rental rates for sub-compacts to luxury cars range from $18-$70 per day to $90-$350 per week. For rentals, availability and more information, contact any of the following: *Alamo,* (800) 327-9633; *Avis,* (800) 831-8000; *Budget,* (800) 527-0700; *Dollar,* (808) 944-1544; *Hertz,* (800) 654-3131; *National,* (800) 227-7368; *Sunshine of Hawaii,* (808) 836-0319; *Thrifty,* (808) 367-2277; *Tropical,* (800) 678-6000; or *Waikiki Rent-A-Car,* (808) 946-2181.

By Taxi. The following taxi companies service the island: *Aloha State Cab,* (808) 847-3566; *Alpha Hawaii Taxi & Tours,* (808) 923-1111; *Americabs,* (808) 521-6680; *Charley's Taxi & Tours,* (808) 531-1333; *Hawaii Kai Taxi Airport Express,* (808) 396-8294; *Kaimuki AA Taxi,* (808) 737-8008; *Royal Taxi & Tour,* (808) 944-5513; *Sida of Hawaii,* (808) 836-0011; *Varsity Taxi,* (808) 947-2008. Typically, taxi fares from the Honolulu Airport to Waikiki are $12-$15.

By Trolley. *Waikiki Trolley,* (808) 596-2199, offers a regularly-scheduled service, with stops every 15 minutes, at all major tourist attractions and shopping centers. The trolley fare is $18.00 adults and $8.00 children for an all-day pass.

Oahu   69

ACCOMMODATIONS

Honolulu

Best Western-The Plaza Hotel. *$90-$120.* 3253 N. Nimitz Hwy., Honolulu; (808) 836-3636/(800) 528-1234. 274-unit hotel, located near Honolulu airport. TV, phones and air conditioning; also pool, shops, meetings rooms, restaurant and cocktail lounge. Handicapped facilities.

Pacific Marina Inn. *$85-$100.* 2628 Waiwai Lp., Honolulu; (808) 836-1131/(800) 548-8040. 110 units, with TV, phones and air conditioning. Pool, restaurant and cocktail lounge. Located near airport.

Pagoda Hotel. *$62-$88.* 1525 Rycroft St., Honolulu; (808) 941-6611/(800) 367-6060. 360 units, with TV, phones, refrigerators, air conditioning; some kitchens available. Pool, shops, meeting rooms, restaurants and cocktail lounge. Handicapped facilities.

Waikiki

Ala Moana Hotel. *$140-$195.* 410 Atkinson Dr., Honolulu; (808) 955-4811/(800) 367-6025. 1172 units; TV, phones, air conditioning. Pool, shops, restaurant and cocktail lounge; also meeting rooms available. Handicapped facilities.

Aston at the Waikiki Banyan. *$130-$180.* 201 Ohua Ave., Honolulu; (808) 922-0555/(800) 922-7866. Condominium complex with 313 units with TV, phones, air conditioning, and kitchens. Pool, tennis court and shops on premises. Daily maid service.

Aston Island Colony. *$77-$120.* 445 Seaside Ave., Honolulu; (808) 923-2345/(800) 922-7866. Situated in Waikiki. 460 hotel units; TV, phones, refrigerators, and air conditioning. Pool, shops, restaurant and cocktail lounge.

Aston Waikiki Beach Tower. *$230-$335.* 2470 Kalakaua Ave., Honolulu; (808) 926-6400/(800) 922-7866. 85 beachfront condominium units; TV, phones, air conditioning, kitchens. Pool, and meeting rooms. Daily maid service. Handicapped facilities.

Aston Waikiki Beachside Hotel. *$160-$290.* 2452 Kalakaua Ave., Honolulu; (808) 931-2100/(800) 922-7866. 79 units with TV, phones, refrigerators and air conditioning. Shops. Daily maid service. Located directly across from Kuhio Beach.

Aston Waikiki Sunset. *$145-$210.* 229 Paoakalani Ave., Honolulu; (808) 922-0511/(800) 922-7866. 330-unit condominium complex. TV, phones, kitchens and air conditioning; pool, tennis court, restaurant. Daily maid service.

The Breakers Hotel. *$91-$125.* 250 Beach Walk, Honolulu; (808) 923-3181/(800) 426-0494. 64 units with TV, phones, air conditioning, and kitchen facilities. Also pool, bar and grill, and restaurant and cocktail lounge. Handicapped facilities.

Coconut Plaza. *$180-$225.* 450 Lewers St., Honolulu; (808) 923-8828/(800) 882-9696. 79-unit hotel, located in central Waikiki. TV, phones, kitchenettes, and air conditioning; pool, restaurant and cocktail lounge. Complimentary breakfast. Handicapped facilities.

Colony Surf Hotel. *$175-$285 condo units, $225-$275 hotel rooms.* 2895 Kalakaua Ave., Honolulu; (808) 924-3111/(800) 777-1700. Beachfront hotel and condominium complex with 150 units with TV, phones, and air conditioning. Beauty salon, restaurants and cocktail lounge. Handicapped facilities.

Diamond Head Beach Hotel. *$126-$146.* 2947 Kalakaua Ave., Honolulu; (808) 922-1928. 53-unit oceanfront hotel. TV, phones, some refrigerators. Complimentary continental breakfast. Daily maid service.

Aston at the Pacific Monarch. *$145-$175.* 142 Uluniu Ave., Honolulu; (808) 923-9805/(800) 321-2588. 168 units, with TV, phones, and air conditioning. Pool, meeting rooms. Handicapped facilities. Located near beach.

Coral Reef Hotel. *$135-$160.* 2299 Kuhio Ave., Honolulu; (808) 922-1262. 247 units; TV, phones, refrigerators, air conditioning. Also pool, shops, restaurant and cocktail lounge.

Halekulani. *$340-$440.* 2199 Kalia Rd., Honolulu; (808) 923-2311/(800) 323-7500. 456-unit, luxury beachfront resort. Facilities include swimming pool, fitness room, beauty salon, shops, meeting rooms, restaurants and cocktail lounge. Handicapped facilities.

Hawaii Prince Hotel Waikiki. *$200-$550.* 100 Holomoana St., Honolulu; (808) 956-1111/(800) 321-6248. Full-service oceanfront hotel, with 521 rooms and suites. Pool, shops, beauty salon, meeting rooms, and restaurant and cocktail lounge on premises. Handicapped facilities.

Hawaiian Monarch. *$109-$141.* 444 Niu St., Honolulu; (808) 949-3911/(800) 535-0085. 300 units with TV, phones, refrigerators, and air conditioning. Pool, shops, meeting rooms. Located a few blocks from the beach.

Hawaiian Regent Hotel. *$165-$290.* 2552 Kalakaua Ave., Honolulu; (808) 922-6611/(800) 367-5370. 1,346-unit, luxury beachfront hotel, with swimming pools, tennis court, shops, beauty salon, meeting rooms, restaurants and cocktail lounge. Handicapped facilities.

Hawaiian Waikiki Beach Hotel. *$150-$220.* 2570 Kalakaua Ave., Honolulu; (808) 922-2511/(800) 877-7666. 715-unit hotel, situated directly across from beach. TV, phones, air conditioning; pool, shops, meeting rooms, restaurants and cocktail lounge. Handicapped facilities.

Hawaiiana Hotel. *$139-$159.* 260 Beach Walk, Honolulu; (808) 923-3811/(800) 367-5122. 95 units, with TV, kitchenettes, and air conditioning. Also pool. Daily maid service. Handicapped facilities. Located half block from beach.

Hilton Hawaiian Village. *$199-350.* 2005 Kalia Rd., Honolulu; (808) 949-4321/(800) HILTONS. Beachfront resort with 2,540 luxury rooms and suites. Hotel facilities include swimming pool, health club and spa, beauty salon, shops, meeting rooms, restaurants and cocktail lounge. Handicapped facilities.

Aston Honolulu Prince. *$90-$140.* 415 Nahua St., Honolulu; (808) 922-1616/(800) 922-7866. 125 units; TV, phones, refrigerators and air conditioning. Beauty salon, shops, restaurant. Handicapped facilities.

Hyatt Regency Waikiki. *$270-$340.* 2424 Kalakaua Ave., Honolulu; (808) 923-1234/(800) 233-1234. Full-service, luxury oceanfront hotel, with 1,230 rooms and suites. Facilities include pool, shops, meeting rooms, restaurant and cocktail lounge. Handicapped facilities.

Ilikai Hotel. *$140-$185.* 1777 Ala Moana Blvd., Honolulu; (808) 949-3811/(800) 367-8434. 800-unit hotel overlooking the Ala Wai Yacht Harbor. TV, phones, air conditioning; some kitchens. Pool, tennis courts, exercise facility, beauty salon, shops, meeting rooms, restaurant and cocktail lounge.

Ilima Hotel. *$115-$130.* 445 Nohonani St., Honolulu; (808) 923-1877/(800) 801-9366. 99 units with TV, phones and air conditioning. Also pool and restaurant and cocktail lounge on premises. Handicapped facilities.

Imperial of Waikiki. *$89-$179.* 205 Lewers St., Honolulu; (808) 923-1827/(800) 745-7666. 110 units in condominium complex, half block from beach. TV, phones, air conditioning, pool, restaurant and cocktail lounge. Daily maid service.

Inn on the Park. *$98-$123.* 1920 Ala Moana Blvd., Honolulu; (808) 946-8355/(800) 367-5004. 134-unit hotel, situated close to the beach. TV, phones, refrigerators, air conditioning. Shops. Daily maid service.

Kahala Mandarin Oriental Hawaii. *$295-$440.* 5000 Kahala Ave.,

Honolulu; (808) 739-8888/(800) 367-2525. Full-service, luxury beachfront resort hotel, with 370 rooms and suites. Facilities include pool and health club, tennis courts, and restaurants and cocktail lounge. Handicapped facilities.

Kaulana Kai Hotel. *$130-$180.* 2425 Kuhio Ave., Honolulu; (808) 922-7777/(800) 367-5666. 90 units; TV, phones, refrigerators, air conditioning. Also pool, sauna and whirlpool. Daily maid service. Located two blocks from beach.

Kuhio Village Resort. *$97-$130.* 2463 Kuhio Ave., Honolulu; (808) 926-0641/(800) 367-5004. 140 units with TV, phones and air conditioning. Shops, meeting rooms, restaurants and cocktail lounge. Located 1½ blocks from beach.

New Otani Kaimana Beach Hotel. *$120-$240.* 2863 Kalakaua Ave., Honolulu; (808) 923-1555. 125-unit hotel located on the beach. TV, phones, refrigerators, and air conditioning; also beauty salon, shops, meeting rooms, restaurants and cocktail lounge.

Ocean Resort Hotel Waikiki. *$75-$125.* 175 Paoakalani Ave., Honolulu; (808) 922-3861/(800) 367-2317. 451 units with TV and phones; some units with kitchens. Pools, shops, meeting rooms, restaurant and cocktail lounge. Located 1½ blocks from beach.

Outrigger Ala Wai Terrace. *$85-$100.* 1547 Ala Wai Blvd., Honolulu; (808) 949-7384/(800) 733-7777. 239 units, with TV, phones and air conditioning. Daily maid service.

Outrigger Coral Seas. *$75-$130.* 250 Lewers St., Honolulu; (808) 923-3881/(800) 733-7777. 109 units with TV, phones and air conditioning. Also shops, restaurant and cocktail lounge on premises. Located close to beach.

Outrigger East Hotel. *$110-$275.* 150 Kaiulani Ave., Honolulu; (808) 922-5353/(800) 733-7777. 445 units; TV, phones, air conditioning. Pool, beauty salon, shops, meeting rooms, restaurants and cocktail lounges. One block from beach.

Outrigger Edgewater Hotel. *$78-$98.* 2168 Kalia Rd., Honolulu; (808) 922-6424/(800) 733-7777. 184 units, with TV, phones and air conditioning; some units with kitchens. Pool, shops, beauty salon, restaurants and cocktail lounge on premises. Close to beach.

Outrigger Hobron Hotel. *$65-$140.* 343 Hobron Lane, Honolulu; (808) 942-7777/(800) 733-7777. 612-unit hotel, located 1½ blocks from the beach. TV, air conditioning, some kitchenettes; pool, health club and spa, shops, restaurant and cocktail lounge.

Outrigger Maile Sky Court. *$65-$150.* 2058 Kuhio Ave., Honolulu; (808) 947-2828/(800) 733-7777. 596 units; TV, phones, refrigerators and air conditioning; also some kitchenettes. Pool, beauty salon, health club and spa, cocktail lounge. Located three blocks from beach.

Outrigger Malia Hotel. *$85-$135.* 2211 Kuhio Ave., Honolulu; (808) 923-7621/(800) 733-7777. 328 units with TV, phones, and air conditioning. Also tennis court, health club, shops, restaurant and cocktail lounge. Handicapped facilities.

Outrigger Prince Kuhio. *$125-$205.* 2500 Kuhio Ave., Honolulu; (808) 922-0811/(800) 733-7777. 625 units, with TV, phones and air conditioning. Pool, shops, beauty salon, meeting rooms, restaurants and cocktail lounge. Handicapped facilities.

Outrigger Reef Hotel. *$145-$320.* 2169 Kalia Rd., Honolulu; (808) 923-3111/(800) 733-7777. 885 units with TV, phones, and air conditioning; some kitchenettes available. Also pool, shops, meeting rooms, restaurants and cocktail lounges. Handicapped facilities. Located near beach.

Outrigger Reef Lanais. *$105-$150.* 224 Saratoga Rd., Honolulu; (808) 923-3881/(800) 733-7777. 110-unit hotel, directly across from beach. TV, phones, air conditioning; some kitchens; park and ocean views. Continental breakfast. Restaurant and cocktail lounge on premises. Continental breakfast.

Outrigger Reef Towers. *$85-$130.* 227 Lewers St., Honolulu; (808) 924-8844/(800) 733-7777. 466 units; TV, phones, air conditioning; some kitchens. Pool, beauty salon, shops, restaurant and cocktail lounge. Located near beach.

Outrigger Royal Islander. *$75-$110.* 2164 Kalia Rd., Honolulu; (808) 922-1961/(800) 733-7777. 101-unit hotel, located on the beach. TV, phones, air conditioning. Restaurant.

Outrigger Surf Hotel. *$78-$125.* 2280 Kuhio Ave., Honolulu; (808) 922-5777/(800) 733-7777. 251 units, with TV, phones, air conditioning, and kitchens. Also pool, shops, restaurant and cocktail lounge. Two blocks from beach.

Outrigger Village. *$85-$115.* 240 Lewers St., Honolulu; (808) 923-3881/(800) 733-7777. 440 units; TV, phones, air conditioning, some kitchens. Pool, shops, restaurant and cocktail lounge. Located one block from beach.

Outrigger Waikiki Hotel. *$160-$500.* 2335 Kalakaua Ave., Honolulu; (808) 923-0711/(800) 733-7777. 530-unit hotel, located on the beach. TV, phones, air conditioning; pool, health club and spa, shops, meeting rooms, restaurants and cocktail lounges. Handicapped facilities.

Outrigger Waikiki Surf. *$65-$115.* 2200 Kuhio Ave., Honolulu; (808) 923-7671/(800) 733-7777. 302 units, with TV, phones, air conditioning, and some kitchens. Also pool, shops and cocktail lounge on premises. Three blocks from beach.

Outrigger Waikiki Surf East. *$75-$125.* 422 Royal Hawaiian Ave., Honolulu; (808) 923-7671/(800) 733-7777. 102 units; TV, phones, air conditioning, kitchens. Also pool. Located three blocks from beach.

Outrigger Waikiki Tower. *$90-$145.* 200 Lewers St., Honolulu; (808) 922-6424/(800) 733-7777. 439-unit hotel, across from beach. TV, phones, air conditioning; some kitchens. Pool, shops, beauty salon, restaurants and cocktail lounge.

Outrigger West Hotel. *$85-$115.* 2330 Kuhio Ave., Honolulu; (808) 922-5022/(800) 733-7777. 663 units, with TV, phones, air conditioning; some kitchens. Also pool, shops, meeting rooms, restaurants and cocktail lounges. Close to beach.

Pacific Beach Hotel. *$180-$280.* 2490 Kalakaua Ave., Honolulu; (808) 922-1233/(800) 367-6060. Oceanfront hotel with 850 rooms and suites with TV, phones and air conditioning. Also pool, tennis court, shops, meeting rooms, restaurant and cocktail lounge on premises.

Doubletree Waikiki. *$115-$180.* 1956 Ala Moana Blvd., Honolulu; (808) 941-7275/(800) 367-6070. 310 units with TV, phones and air conditioning. Pool, health club and spa, shops, meeting rooms, restaurants and cocktail lounge. Handicapped facilities. Located near beach.

Park Shore Hotel. *$150-$235.* 2586 Kalakaua Ave., Honolulu; (808) 923-0411/(800) 367-2377. 227 units; TV, phones, air conditioning. Pool, shops, restaurants and cocktail lounge. Handicapped facilities. Located across from beach.

Queen Kapiolani Hotel. *$150-$180.* 150 Kapahulu Ave., Honolulu; (808) 922-1941/(800) 367-5004. 314 units with TV, phones and air conditioning; some kitchens. Pool, shops, meeting rooms, restaurants and cocktail lounge. Half block from beach.

Sheraton Royal Hawaiian Hotel. *$310-$450.* 2259 Kalakaua Ave., Honolulu; (808) 923-7311/(800) 325-3535. Luxury beachfront hotel, with 525 rooms and suites with TV, phones and air conditioning. Other facilities include a pool, shops, beauty salon, meeting rooms, restaurants and cocktail lounge. Handicapped facilities.

Sheraton Moana Surfrider. *$229-$269.* 2365 Kalakaua Ave., Honolulu; (808) 922-3111/(800) 325-3535. 786-unit beachfront hotel. TV, phones, air conditioning; pool, beauty salon, shops, meeting rooms, restaurants and cocktail lounge. Handicapped facilities.

Sheraton Princess Kaiulani Hotel. *$145-$185.* 120 Kaiulani Ave., Honolulu; (808) 922-5811/(800) 325-3535. 1,150 units, with TV, phones, and

Oahu

73

air conditioning. Pool, shops, meeting rooms, restaurant and cocktail lounge. Handicapped facilities. Located across from beach.

Waikiki Beachcomber Hotel. *$135-$185.* 2300 Kalakaua Ave., Honolulu; (808) 922-4646/(800) 622-4646. 498 units; TV, phones, refrigerators, air conditioning. Pool, beauty salon, shops, meeting rooms, restaurants and cocktail lounge. Handicapped facilities. Located across from beach.

Aston Waikiki Circle Hotel. *$135-$175.* 2464 Kalakaua Ave., Honolulu; (808) 923-1571. 100 units overlooking ocean. TV, phones, air conditioning; beauty salon, restaurants and cocktail lounge. Handicapped facilities.

Waikiki Gateway. *$85-$99.* 2070 Kalakaua Ave., Honolulu; (808) 921-3204/(800) 247-1903. 185 units with TV, phones and air conditioning. Also pool, shops, restaurant and cocktail lounge on premises.

Waikiki Grand Hotel. *$119-$149.* 134 Kapahulu Ave., Honolulu; (808) 921-1511/(800) 535-0085. 115 units, with TV, phones, refrigerators, and air conditioning. Pool, shops, restaurant and cocktail lounge adjacent. Half block from beach; close to zoo, aquarium and park.

Waikiki Joy Hotel. *$108-$155.* 320 Lewers St., Honolulu; (808) 923-2300/(800) 733-5569. 93 units with TV, stereos, refrigerators, jacuzzis, and air conditioning. Complimentary breakfast. Pool, restaurant and cocktail lounge. Handicapped facilities. Located two blocks from beach.

Waikiki Parc Hotel. *$140-$240.* 2233 Helumoa Rd., Honolulu; (808) 921-7272/(800) 422-0450. 298-unit hotel, located across from beach. TV, phones, air conditioning; pool, shops, restaurant. Handicapped facilities. In Waikiki across from the beach. 298 units; air conditioning, room phone and TV. Swimming pool. Shops and restaurant. Wheelchair access.

Waikiki Parkside Hotel. *$95-$145.* 1850 Ala Moana Blvd., Honolulu; (808) 955-1567/(800) 237-9666. 250 units, with TV, phones, balconies, and air conditioning. Pool, shops, meeting rooms, restaurants and cocktail lounge. Handicapped facilities.

Waikiki Prince Hotel. *$65-$100.* 2431 Prince Edward St., Honolulu; (808) 922-1544. 30 units with TV and air conditioning; some kitchens. Handicapped facilities.

Waikiki Resort Hotel. *$118-$158.* 2460 Koa Ave., Honolulu; (808) 922-4911/(800) 367-5116. 296 units; TV, phones, air conditioning. Pool, shops, meeting rooms, restaurants and cocktail lounge. Located across from beach.

Waikiki Royal Suites. *$189-$359.* 255 Beach Walk, Honolulu; (808) 926-5641/(800) 535-0085. 47 condominium units with TV, phones, kitchens, and air conditioning. Shops, and restaurant. Daily maid service. One block from beach.

Waikiki Sand Villa Hotel. *$85-$168.* 2375 Ala Wai Blvd., Honolulu; (808) 922-4744/(800) 247-1903. 223-unit hotel overlooking Waikiki's Ala Wai Canal. TV, phones, refrigerators and air conditioning; also shops, restaurant and cocktail lounge.

Aston Waikiki Terrace Hotel. *$103-$159.* 2945 Kalakaua Ave., Honolulu; (808) 955-6000/(800) 445-8811. 250 units; TV, phones, refrigerator, air conditioning, private balconies. Pool, health club and spa, shops, meeting rooms, restaurants and cocktail lounge. Handicapped facilities. Two blocks from beach.

North Shore

Turtle Bay Hilton & Country Club. *$160-$230.* 57-091 Kamehameha Hwy., Kahuku; (808) 293-8811/(800) HILTONS. 486-room oceanfront resort hotel, with golf course, tennis courts, pool, health club, beauty salon, shops, meeting rooms, restaurants and cocktail lounge. Handicapped facilities.

74 Oahu

BED & BREAKFASTS

(Reservations for bed and breakfast inns on the island can be made centrally through *All Islands Bed & Breakfast,* 823 Kainui Dr., Kailua, (808) 236-2342/(800) 542-0344; or *Pacific-Hawaii Bed & Breakfast & Vacation Rental Agency,* 970 N. Kalaheo Ave., Suite A-218, Kailua; (808) 262-6026/(800) 999-6026.)

Akamai Bed & Breakfast. *$75.* Kailua; (808) 261-2227/(800) 642-5366. Contemporary Hawaiian house with two large guest rooms with private baths and private entrances; individual kitchenettes with refrigerators. Also TV and phone in room. Pool and lanai. Located close to Kailua Beach.

Kahana Kai. *$100-$300.* 53-103 Kamehameha Hwy., Pualuu; (808) 237-8431/(800) 462-4805. One large ocean view suite and 3 garden view rooms, all with private baths. Continental breakfast.

Manoa Valley Inn. *$99-$190.* 2001 Vancouver Rd., Honolulu; (808) 947-6017. Historic country inn with 8 suites, situated on luch half-acre estate close to Waikiki. Continental breakfast and complimentary evening wine.

Paradise Palms Bed & Breakfast. *$60-$65.* 804 Mokapu Rd., Kailua; (808) 254-4234. 2 guest rooms with private entrances, kitchenettes and private baths. Also, air-conditioning, TV and phone. Close to Kailua Beach.

Sheffield House. *$50-$90.* 131 Kuulei Rd., Kailua; (808) 262-0721. 1 guest room, and one 1-bedroom apartment, each with private bath. Continental breakfast. Located close to Kailua Beach.

VACATION RENTALS

Bali Hai Treasures. (800) 688-2254. A variety of vacation homes and condominiums are available. Rates from $100.00 per night.

Estates at Turtle Bay. P.O. Box 366, Kahuku; (808) 293-0600. Fully-equipped studio apartments, 1-, 2- and 3-bedroom condominiums. Pool, golf and tennis available. Rates from $100.00 per night.

Go Condo Hawaii. (800) 452-3463. Represent several condominium complexes in Waikiki. Rates from $80.00 per night.

Turtle Bay Condominiums. P.O. Box 248, Kahuku; (808) 293-2800. Fully-equipped studio apartments, and 1- and 2-bedroom condominiums. Also some beachfront houses. Swimming pool, golf and tennis. Rates from $100.00 per night.

Utopia Vacation Connection. 1314 S. King St., Suite 706, Honolulu; (808) 593-0066. Variety of beachfront homes and condominiums are available. Rates from $110.00 per night.

Oahu 75

SEASONAL EVENTS

January

First Weekend. *Narcissus Festival.* Month-long celebration of the Chinese New Year, held throughout the island. Festivities include the "Queen Pageant," coronation ball, fashion show, and Chinese art and cooking demonstrations. For a schedule of events and more information, call the Chinese Chamber of Commerce at (808) 533-3181.

Second Weekend. *Japanese New Year.* At the Japanese Cultural Center, Honolulu. Events including ikebana and bonsai exhibits; also Japanese food and crafts. For more information, call (808) 945-7633.

Third Weekend. *Ala Wai Challenge.* Sports competition, featuring traditional Hawaiian sports such as outrigger canoe races and a tug-of-war. Events take place at Ala Wai Park in Waikiki. For complete schedule, call (808) 923-1802. *Morey Boogie World Championships.* Held at Ehukai Beach Park on the island's North Shore. Popular annual bodyboarding competition, featuring 80 men and women from 20 different countries, competing for $20,000 in prize money, at the world-famous "Banzai Pipeline." For more information, call (808) 396-8342.

February

First Weekend. *NFL Pro Bowl.* At the Aloha Stadium, Honolulu. Annual all-star professional football game, between the American and National conferences. For tickets and more information, call (808) 486-9300. *Chinese New Year Celebrations.* In Chinatown, Honolulu. Annual celebration featuring lion dances, music and fireworks. Call (808) 533-3181 for complete schedule.

Second Weekend. *Hawaiian Open Golf Tournament.* Held at the Waialae Country Club Golf Course in Honolulu. PGA event, featuring professional golfers, with a $1.2-million prize. For more information, call (808) 526-1232/ 831-5400. *Buffalo's Big Board Surfing Classic.* Makaha Beach, Makaha. Surfing contest, featuring early-day wooden longboards. Also tandem surfing and canoe surfing. More information on (808) 696-0120.

Third Weekend. *Great Aloha Run.* Held in Honolulu. Annual 8.2-mile run, beginning at the Aloha Tower on the Honolulu waterfront and ending at the Aloha Stadium. This is one of Hawaii's most popular running events, featuring 35,000 runners. (808) 945-3594. *Hawaiian Ladies Open.* Women's golf tournament, held at the Kapolei Golf Course. $600,000 in prize money. For a schedule and more information, call (808) 671-5050.

Fourth Weekend. *Cherry Blossom Festival.* Annual Japanese festival, held during the months of February and March, at various locations throughout the island. Features traditional dance and drama, a cooking show, a culture and crafts fair, and the crowing of a cherry blossom queen in a full court. For a schedule of events, locations, and more information, call the Japanese Junior Chamber of Commerce at (808) 955-2778.

Oahu

March

First Weekend. *Oahu Kite Festival.* Held at the Queen Kapiolani Park in Waikiki. Features individual as well as team kite-flying competitions, with national and international participants. For information, call Kite Fantasy, (808) 922-5483.

Second Weekend. *St. Patricks Day Parade.* Traditional St. Patrick's Day parade, beginning at Fort DeRussy in Waikiki, and ending at the Queen Kapiolani Park. Also party at the end of the parade, at the Hawaiian Waikiki Beach Hotel. For more information, call (808) 521-8693.

May

First Weekend. *Lei Day Celebration.* Celebration of Hawaiian leis, with a state-wide lei-making competition, held at the Queen Kapiolani Park in Honolulu. Features colorful leis, made from flowers, feathers and shells; also crowning of Lei Queen. (808) 266-7654. *Filipino Parade.* Colorful parade down Kalakaua Avenue, from Ala Moana Park to Kapiolani Park. Also live entertainment by Filipino community members, and food and crafts. For more information, call (808) 533-0322.

Second Week. *World Fire-Knife Dance Championships.* At the Polynesian Cultural Center. Top junior and adult fire dancers compete. Call (808) 293-3333 for more information.

Third Weekend. *Bankoh Kayak Challenge.* Annual 38-mile kayak race, beginning at Molokai's Kaluakoi Resort and ending at the Koko Marina, at Hawaii Kai, in East Honolulu. (808) 239-4123.

Fourth Weekend. *Hoomanao Challenge.* 75-mile outrigger sailing canoe race, with 6-man teams. Begins at the Whaler's Village in Ka'anapali, Maui, and ends at Waikiki Beach, Oahu. Party at finish. For more information, call (808) 325-7400.

Fourth Week. *Hawaii Special Olympics Summer Games.* Held at the University of Hawaii in Honolulu. 1,000 Special Olympians from all islands participate in track and field, aquatics, power lifting, softball, and other events. Call (808) 531-1888 for a schedule. *Hawaii State Fair.* Aloha Stadium, Honolulu. Fair begins on Memorial weekend and lasts for four weekends. Features a variety of rides, commercial booths, including food concessions, and entertainment. For more information, call (808) 595-4606. *Warrior Society Pow Wow.* Native dancers and drummers from all over the United States and Canada perform at Kapiolani Park. More information on (808) 947-3306.

June

First Weekend. *King Kamehameha Celebrations.* Held in Honolulu and Waikiki. Annual celebration, honoring Hawaii's first monarch, King Kamehameha I. Festivities include a colorful parade with floral floats, marching bands, drill teams and military units, which begins in downtown Honolulu and winds down King and Richard streets, Ala Moana Boulevard and Kalakaua Avenue, to Queen Kapiolani Park; also awards ceremony and arts and crafts and lei-making demonstrations. For more information, call the King Kamehameha Celebration Commission/State Council on Hawaiian Heritage at (808) 536-6540/(808) 586-0333.

Second Week. *Aloha State Games.* Held at various locations throughout Oahu. Features some 46 different events, including archery, fencing, boxing,

Oahu 77

wrestling, karate, swimming, surfing, yachting, cycling, tennis and basketball, with over 10,000 competitors. More information on (808) 522-0700.

Third Weekend. *King Kamehameha Hula Competition.* At the Blaisdell Arena, Honolulu. Hula competition, featuring ancient and contemporary styles of hula, performed by 30 halau; male, female and individual chants. For more information, call (808) 536-6540/521-2911. *Hard Rock Cafe Rock 'N' Roll 10K Run for the Homeless.* Annual 10K run, from the Honolulu Hard Rock Cafe on Kapiolani Boulevard to Ala Moana Beach Park on Ala Moana Boulevard. Proceeds benefit the homeless in Hawaii. (808) 254-2996. *Professional Championship Rodeo.* Held at the New Town & Country Stables in Waimanalo, on the east shore of the island. International rodeo, with more than 300 contestants and $50,000 in prize money. Features 3 days of Western events, including horse races, bareback riding, roping, and country entertainment. For a schedule of events and more information, call (808) 235-3691.

July

First Week. *Fourth of July.* Independence day parade held in Kailua, on Kainalu Drive, featuring floral floats, marching bands and military units. Also fireworks display at Kailua Beach Park and at Ala Moana Beach Park in Honolulu. For more information, call the Kailua Chamber of Commerce at (808) 261-2727. *Walter J. MacFarlane Regatta.* At Waikiki Beach. 30 outrigger canoe races, from the beach to the open ocean and back. Races start at 8.30 a.m., on July 4th.

Second Week. *Transpacific Yacht Race.* Yachts participating in annual race from Los Angeles to Honolulu will cross the finish line off Diamond Head. Call (808) 946-9061 for daily information.

Third Week. *Bayfest.* At Kaneole Bay. 3-day water sports carnival featuring a variety of water sports, a health and fitness fair, live entertainment, carnival rides, military displays and food concessions. For a complete schedule, call (808) 254-7679. *Prince Lot Hula Festival.* Held at the Moanalua Gardens in Honolulu, commemorating Kamehameha V. Exhibition hula performances, featuring more than a dozen halau; also food concessions, and arts and crafts fair. (808) 839-5334.

Fourth Weekend. *Ukulele Festival.* Held at the Queen Kapiolani Park Bandstand, in Waikiki. Annual Hawaiian music festival, with more than 300 ukulele players performing. More information on (808) 732-3739.

August

Third Weekend. *Duke Kahanamoku Canoe Races.* Men's and women's canoe races take place at Kailua Beach Park. Call (808) 923-1585 for schedule. *Bankoh Ki-Ho'alu.* At Bishop Museum, Honolulu. Celebration of Hawaiian slack key guitar music. Call (808) 239-4336 for more information.

Fourth Weekend. *Kailua Bay Iron Challenge Canoe Race.* Contestants race from Kailua Beach to Moku Lea Island and back. (808) 923-1585.

September

First Weekend. *Queen's Serenade.* Musical tribute to Queen Lili'uokaiani takes place at the Iolani Palace. Call (808) 522-0822 for schedule. *Hawaiian Falsetto Contest.* At Royal Hawaiian Hotel. Singers from all islands compete. (808) 545-1771.

Second Week. *Aloha Festival.* Month-long, island-wide festival begins. Events include floral parades, a steel guitar festival, storytelling, horse racing, lei contests, fishing tournaments and ukelele performances. For complete schedule, call the festival office at (808) 545-1771. Also, on the first night of the festival, the Hilton Hawaiian Village hosts the *King's Jubilee and Festival* with events including a king's procession, flag ceremony, precision rifle drill and fireworks display. Call the hotel on (808) 949-4321 for a detailed schedule.

Third Weekend. *Waikiki Hollaulea.* Largest block party on Oahu. It features live performances at various stages set up in Waikiki; also food booths and lei vendors. (808) 545-1771.

Fourth Weekend. *Bankoh Na Wahine O Hawaii.* At Bishop Museum. Many of Hawaii's outstanding women performers present traditional and contemporary music and dance performances. Call (808) 239-4336 for a complete schedule.

October

First Weekend. *Waimea Falls Park Makahiki Festival.* Waimea Falls Park, on the north shore of the island. Features hula competitions, dancing, entertainment, Hawaiian sporting events, food, arts and crafts. (808) 638-8511.

Second Weekend. *SOEST Open House.* Held at the School of Ocean and Earth Science and Technology at the University of Hawaii. Activities include hands-on learning activities, laboratory tours and displays of high-tech equipment. *Bankoh Molokai Hoe.* Men's 40.8-mile outrigger canoe race, from Molokai to Oahu, finishing at Fort DeRussy Beach, Waikiki. (808) 261-6615.

Third Week. *Orchid, Plant & Flower Show.* Four-day show, takes place at the Neal Blaisdell Exhibition Hall. This is Hawaii's largest orchid show, featuring orchid displays and also African violets, bonsai plants, cacti and succulents, and bromeliads. Plant sale, lectures, and demonstrations. Call (808) 545-4300 for more information.

November

First Week. *Ho'i Maii Ka Pilo - Annual World Invitational Hula Festival.* Takes place at the Waikiki Shell in Queen Kapiolani Park, Honolulu. Competition featuring halau hula from different countries around the world. Call (808) 486-3185 for schedule.

Second Week. *Hawaii International Film Festival.* Showcases 125 films from Asia, the Pacific and the U.S., emphasizing the cross-cultural diversity of the Pacific Rim. Screenings are held at various locations throughout the island, and there is no admission fee to the films. For a schedule and locations, call (800) 752-8193 or (808) 528-3458. *G-Shock Triple Crown of Surfing.* Held at Ali'i Beach Park, Haleiwa, and other locations. Events continue through December 20th, when the new men's and women's world champions are named. Includes pro-surfing championships, women's pro-surfing championships and junior surfing championships. More information on (808) 637-6376.

Third Week. *Birthday Celebration for a King.* At Iolani Palace. Annual commemoration of King Kalakua's birthday. Call (808) 522-0832.

Fourth Week. *Triple Crown of Surfing.* Week-long surfing competition, held at Sunset Beach on Oahu's North Shore. Events include the Rip Curl World Cup of Surfing and the Quicksilver Roxy Pro.

Oahu   79

December

Second Week. *Chiemsee Gerry Lopez Pipe Masters.* Oldest professional surfing competition in the United States. Takes place at the Banzai Pipeline, Ehukai Beach. Call (808) 638-5024 for schedule. *Candlelight Christmas at Mission Houses.* Experience a 19th-century holiday celebration at the Mission Houses Museum in Honolulu. More information on (808) 531-0481. *Honolulu Marathon.* Premier U.S. marathon, with more than 34,000 runners participating. Begins at the Aloha Tower at the Honolulu waterfront, then heads east to Hawaii Kai in East Honolulu, and ends at Kapiolani Park in Waikiki. For more information, call the Honolulu Marathon Association at (808) 734-7200.

Fourth Week. *Jeep Eagle Aloha Bowl.* Post-season football game, held at the Aloha Stadium in Honolulu, on Christmas Day. Features two of the top-ranked NCAA teams. For tickets and more information, call (808) 947-4141. *First Night Honolulu.* New Year's Eve celebration, covering 25 city blocks. Approximately 1,500 musicians, dancers, actors, jugglers, magicians and mimes provide entertainment for this alcohol-free event. (808) 532-3131.

PLACES OF INTEREST

Honolulu

Iolani Palace. 300 South King St., Honolulu; (808) 522-0832. Historic Hawaiian royal palace, built in 1882 by King Kalakaua, in the ornate Italian Renaissance architectural style, and restored in 1978, at a cost of $6 million. This is the nation's only royal palace, and also the site of the overthrow and imprisonment of the last Hawaiian monarch, Queen Liliuokalani, in 1893. Tours of the palace include the *Grand Hall* with its sweeping koa staircase and cedar walls adorned with portraits of Hawaiian and European royal personages; the *Royal Dining Room*, with its European-design period furnishings; the *King's Library*, with antique, 19th-century desk and chairs, old books and photographs, and one of the island's first telephones; the *royal bedrooms* of King Kalakaua and Queen Liliuokalani; and the *Throne Room*, with the original thrones of the king and queen. Open Tues.-Sat., 9 a.m.- 2.15 p.m.; tours by reservation. Admission fee: $8.00 adults; $3.00 children (ages 5-12); children under 5 not permitted in the palace.

Iolani Barracks. Located adjacent to Iolani Palace, off Richards St.; (808) 522-0832. Old grey-stone building, dating from 1870, originally built during the reign of King Kamehameha V to house the Royal Guards. The barracks were originally built on the site of the present-day State Capitol building, behind the palace on Beretania Street, and moved to present location in 1965. Now houses ticket office for Iolani Palace tours. Open Mon.-Sat., 8-3.30.

Queen Liliuokalani Statue. Located behind Iolani Palace, on palace grounds. 8-foot bronze statue of Queen Liliuokalani, Hawaii's last monarch, dedicated in 1982. The statue is the work of Boston sculptor Marianne Pineda.

Royal Coronation Bandstand. Situated on palace grounds, near the corner of South King and Richards Sts. Bandstand-cum-coronation stand, built in 1883, and notable as the site of the coronation of King Kalakaua and Queen Kapiolani. The bandstand is now used by the Royal Hawaiian Band, which performs here every Friday.

Aliiolani Hale. Corner of South King and Mililani Sts., across from Iolani Palace. Historic building, originally built in 1874 by King Kamehameha V to house the Hawaiian parliament and courts, and now home to the judiciary—the official Judiciary Building. Also of interest, directly in front of Aliiolani Hale is the *Kamehameha Statue*, a 30-foot bronze statue of Hawaii's first great monarch, Kamehameha I. The statue is one of Hawaii's most photographed monuments.

Hawaii State Library. 478 King St. (cnr. Punchbowl St.), Honolulu; (808) 548-4775. This is the main branch of the state library system, housed in a lovely, early 1900s building with a central courtyard. Features a rare collection of books on the history of Hawaii. Open Mon.-Sat., 9-5.

Kawaiahao Church. 957 Punchbowl St. (cnr. South King St.); (808) 522-1333. Hawaii's oldest church, established in 1820, and built in 1842, from 14,000 slabs of coral, some of them weighing more than 1,000 pounds each. This was also the church of Hawaiian royalty, where kings and queens worshipped and were crowned, married, and given their last rites as well. Also on the grounds is the *Lunalilo Mausoleum*, the final resting place of King Lunalilo, built in 1879. The church is open to the public Mon.-Fri., 9-12.

Mission Houses Museum. 553 South King St., Honolulu; (808) 531-0481. The museum comprises three buildings: a New England-style *wood-frame house*, one of the oldest American-style buildings in the islands, dating from 1821; the *Chamberlain House*, formerly a storehouse for missionaries and now restored, with its original, period furnishings; and the *Print House*, which has on display a 19th-century printing press—one of Hawaii's oldest—on which early missionaries printed the first English-Hawaiian translations of the Bible. Open Tues.-Sat. 9-4, and Sun. 12-4. Admission fee: $5.00 adults, $4.00 seniors, $1.00 children (ages 4-18).

Honolulu Hale (City Hall). Located on South King St., near the corner of Punchbowl St., across from the Kawaiahao Church. Spanish Renaissance-style building, with a terra-cotta-tiled open courtyard, designed by noted Honolulu architect C.W. Dickey, and built in 1927. Open Mon.-Fri., 9-5.

State Capitol. Located on South Beretania St., between Punchbowl and Richards Sts.; (808) 548-5420. One of Honolulu's most interesting modern structures, built in 1969, at a cost of around $25 million. Features a central court-yard, and surrounding reflecting pools. Also on the grounds, at the front of the building, is the *Father Damien Statue*, dedicated to the Belgian priest who devoted much of his life to the lepers of Molokai. The State Capitol is open to public viewing; the legislature is in session Jan.-May, and the legislative chambers are open Mon.-Fri., 8-4.30.

Washington Place. 320 South Beretania Street, Honolulu. Splendid, white colonial mansion, situated on landscaped grounds, across from the State Capitol. Originally built in 1847 by American sea captain John Dominis, father-in-law of Queen Liliuokalani, and named after George Washington. The mansion is now the official residence of the governor of Hawaii. Not open to public, but may be viewed from Beretania Street.

St. Andrews Cathedral. Cnr. Alakea and Beretania Sts.; (808) 524-2822. Historic Episcopal church, founded in 1862 by King Kamehameha IV and his wife, Queen Emma. Features cut stones and stained-glass windows imported from England. The church is named for the fact that Kamehameha died on St. Andrew's Day, in 1863, a year after its founding. Open daily, 6.30 a.m.-6 p.m.

Our Lady of Peace Cathedral. Located on Beretania St., at the Fort Street Mall. The church dates from 1840, and is built from coral blocks cut from a nearby reef. Features a bell tower.

Chinatown. Colorful, 38-acre quarter, adjoining to the west of downtown Honolulu, bounded by Nu'uanu Avenue and North Beretania, North King and River streets. Originally established in the early 1800s, and largely rebuilt at the turn of the century. Features lively sidewalk markets, scores of Chinese restaurants

Oahu

and diners, noodle factories, fabric stores, handicraft emporiums, souvenir shops, and, along a stretch of *North Hotel Street*, dance halls, porn shops, pool halls, gambling dens and cheap bars. Places of particular interest here include the old *Oahu Market*, an open-air produce market at the corner of Kekaulike and North King streets, established in 1904; the pink-and-green *Wo Fat Restaurant* on North Hotel Street, dating from 1882; the *River Street Pedestrian Mall*, which comprises a section of River Street, between Beretania and Kukui streets; the *lei shops* along Beretania Street, between Smith and Maunakea streets; and the *Kuan Yin Temple*, the oldest Chinese temple in Honolulu, dating from the 1880s, and located on North Vineyard Boulevard.

Foster Botanic Garden. 180 North Vineyard Blvd., Honolulu; (808) 522-7060. 20-acre tropical botanical garden with more than 4,000 species of tropical flowers, plants and trees from all over the world, including native Asian and South Pacific tropical trees, such as the Bo Tree, Chinese Banyan Tree, Tropical Almond Tree, Loulu Palm, Yoke-Wood Tree, Queensland Kauri Tree and Pili Nut Tree, among others. Open daily, 9-4; admission fee: $3.00 for Hawaii residents, $5.00 for non-residents.

Honolulu Academy of Arts. 900 South Beretania St., Honolulu; (808) 532-8700/532-8701. Prestigious art museum, housed in the former home of art collector Mrs. Montagne Cooke, dating from 1927. Comprises 30 individual galleries, surrounded by garden courtyards, featuring a splendid collection of contemporary and ancient art—Oriental, American and European—including works of Gauguin, Van Gogh and Picasso, and Japanese ceramics and paintings, antiques from the Ming and Ching dynasties, and original Hawaiian, South Pacific and rare African art. Open Tues.-Sat. 10-4.30, Sun. 1-5. Admission: $5.00 adults.

Royal Mausoleum State Monument. 2261 Nu'uanu Avenue, Honolulu. Burial place of Hawaiian royalty, where Kings Kamehameha II, III, IV, V and Kalakaua, as well as Queen Liliuokalani, are buried. The mausoleum, now a state historic monument, is housed in a Gothic-style, Latin cross-shaped structure, built between 1863 and 1865. Open to public viewing, Mon.-Fri., 8-4.30; free admission.

Bishop Museum. 1525 Bernice St., Honolulu; (808) 847-3511. This is Hawaii's most famous museum, frequently referred to as the "Smithsonian of the Pacific," which houses one of the world's greatest collections of Hawaiian cultural and natural history artifacts. referred to Hawaii's most famous museum, housing the world's largest collection of Hawaiian cultural and natural history artifacts, frequently referred to as the "Smithsonian of the Pacific." The museum was founded in 1899, and dedicated to Bernice Pauahi Bishop, a Hawaiian princess of the Kamehameha dynasty, who personally collected many of the artifacts on display here. At the center of the museum is the *Hawaiian Hall*, where exhibits include 26 original feather cloaks of Hawaiian kings—including those worn by King Kamehameha I—as well as feather helmets, leis, carved calabashes and wooden tikis, temple drums, 19th-century Hawaiian weapons, royal thrones and royal crowns. There is also a *Polynesian Hall* here, which has displays centered around the history and culture of Pacific Polynesia, including several collections of archaeological artifacts from Polynesian islands; and the *Hawaiian Hall of Natural History*, featuring exhibits depicting Hawaii's geological formation. Another, the *Hall of Discovery*, has hands-on science and Pacific culture educational exhibits for children. Besides which there are a *planetarium* and *observatory* on the premises, and a native Hawaiian culture and arts program, which includes lei-making, hala-weaving, quilting and hula demonstrations and Hawaiian music. Restaurant and gift shop on premises. Open daily 9-5; admission fee: $14.95 adults, $11.95 children (ages 6-12).

National Memorial Cemetary of the Pacific (Punchbowl Crater). 2177 Puowaina Dr., Honolulu; (808) 541-1430. Situated on the floor of the Punchbowl Crater—a 75,000-year-old extinct volcano—encompassing 112½ acres. Contains 28,000 graves of military personnel killed in the Pacific theater in World War II and the Korean War. Also features a marble-walled monument, the "Garden of the Missing," which has inscribed on it the names of the men and women who served in the South Pacific during World War II and the Korean and Vietnam wars, but whose remains were not recovered or who were missing in action or buried at sea. Open daily, 8-5.30.

Dole Cannery Square. 650 Iwilei Rd., Honolulu; (808) 528-2236. Formerly the site of the turn-of-the-century Dole Pineapple Cannery. Now houses a visitor center, with displays centered around the history of the pineapple industry in Hawaii and the pineapple canning process. Also 20-minute video presentation, and garden tour and sampling of fresh pineapple juice. The square also houses a variety of shops and restaurants. Cannery Square is open 9-5 daily; video presentations are featured 9.30-3.30 daily.

Aloha Tower. Located at Pier 9, at the Honolulu Harbor. 10-story tower, built in 1921, and a landmark for those arriving or departing Honolulu by ship. There is an *Observation Deck* on the tenth floor of the tower, reached by taking the escalator to the second floor of Pier 9, then the Observation Elevator to the very top. Observation Deck open 8 a.m.-9 p.m. Free admission.

Hawaii Maritime Center. Located at Pier 7, Honolulu Harbor; (808) 536-6373. Houses a *maritime museum*, devoted to ocean travel, where displays are of canoes, replica ships and sailing vessels; also exhibits centered around Polynesian history, Hawaiian customs and culture, the Hawaiian sandalwood trade, and the history of whaling. The center also has on display, anchored in the harbor, the *Falls of Clyde*, a 266-foot, four-masted, square-rigged 19th-century ship, built in Scotland in 1878; and the *Hokulea*, a 65-foot, double-hulled voyaging canoe, built in 1976 as a replica of the ancient ocean-faring canoes, to educate children in early-day navigational methods. The center is open daily 8.30-5; admission fee: $7.50 adults, $4.50 children (ages 6-17). Free parking at adjacent Pier 6.

Ala Moana Center. Located on Ala Moana Blvd., between Piikoi and Atkinson Sts. Hawaii's largest shopping mall, with over 200 shops, including major department stores such as Sears and Liberty House, several boutiques, and a food court with an assortment of ethnic fast-food restaurants.

Aina Moana Beach Park (Magic Island). Located at the east end of Ala Moana Beach Park, off Ala Moana Blvd. The "island" park comprises a largely grassy, 36-acre man-made peninsula, bordering the Ala Wai Canal, created in 1964. There is a lagoon at the tip of the peninsula, with a protected, crescent-shaped sandy beach which has good, safe swimming conditions, lifeguard, picnic facilities, showers and restrooms. Park hours: 7.45 a.m.-7 p.m.

The Contemporary Museum. 2411 Makiki Heights Dr., Honolulu; (808) 526-0232. Housed in the former home of art collector Mrs. Montagne Cooke, built in 1926. Features a small, permanent collection of contemporary art—post World War II— as well as rotating exhibits. Gift shop and cafe on premises. Open Tues.-Sat. 10-4, Sun. 12-4. Admission fee: $5.00 adults, $3.00 students and seniors, children under 12 free (free admission on 3rd Thursday of each month).

Pu'u Ualakaa State Wayside Park. Situated on Round Top, off Round Top Dr. (which is an extension of Makiki Dr.), some 2½ miles northeast of Honolulu. Hillside park, at an elevation of 1,050 feet, with panoramic views of Honolulu and the Pacific Ocean. Picnic facilities.

Lyon Arboretum. 3860 Manoa Rd., Honolulu; (808) 988-7378. 124-acre arboretum-cum-nursery, situated in the lush Manoa Valley, at the foot of the Koolau Mountains, established in 1918. Features over 5,000 species of indigenous plants, flowers and trees, including a variety of palms, taro, ginger, heliconia and Malaysian rhododendrons. Self-guided tour leads past the flora to "Inspiration Point," which offers an overview of the arboretum and good, all-round views of

Oahu   83

Manoa Valley. The arboretum is now owned and maintained by the University of Hawaii. Open Mon.-Sat. 9-3. $1.00 admission.

Pali Highway

Queen Emma Summer Palace. 2913 Pali Hwy., Honolulu; (808) 595-3167. Off Pali Hwy. (61), 3/4 mile east of Honolulu. Lovely, white colonial mansion, formerly the summer home of Queen Emma, wife of Kamehameha IV. The home was originally built in 1847, and shipped to Hawaii and re-erected. Now fully restored, and maintained as a museum. Houses original, antique koa furniture, portraits of the Hawaiian royal family, and a variety of old Hawaiian artifacts, including 19th-century feather caps, cloaks and tapa bedspreads. Gift shop on premises. Open 8 a.m.-4 p.m. daily; admission fee: $5.00 adults, $1.00 children under 16.

Nu'uanu Pali Lookout. Located on Pali Hwy. (61), 5½ miles east of Honolulu. The lookout is at an elevation of around 1,200 feet, flanked by cliffs that rise vertically, 2,000 to 3,000 feet. Offers spectacular views of the Windward Coast and the coastal communities of Kaneohe and Kailua. The lookout is also the site of an historic battle in 1795, in which defenders of the island of Oahu were driven over the cliffs into the Nu'uanu Valley by the invading forces of Kamehameha I.

Waikiki

Fort DeRussy. Off Kalia Rd., between Ala Moana Blvd. and Saratoga Ave., Waikiki. 42-acre military reserve, originally acquired by the U.S. government in 1904 and used as a rest and recreation center for military personnel since. This is a largely grassy tract, fronted by a 100-yard-wide sandy beach, the Fort DeRussy Beach Park. Also has on it a U.S. Army museum.

US Army Museum. Kalia Rd., at Fort DeRussy, Waikiki; (808) 955-9552. Housed in the old Battery Randolph structure, dating from 1908. Displays are of military exhibits, centered around the history of the U.S. military in Hawaii and the Pacific. Gift shop on premises. Museum hours: 10-4.30, Tues.-Sun. Free admission.

Royal Hawaiian Shopping Center. Located on Kalakaua Ave., near Royal Hawaiian Ave., in Waikiki. This is Waikiki's largest shopping center, three blocks long, and with three levels of shops—gift shops, boutiques, art galleries, jewelry shops and restaurants. Contains over 150 shops and restaurants. Open daily, 9 a.m.-10 p.m.

International Marketplace. Kalakaua Ave., between Dukes Lane and Kaiulani Ave., Waikiki. The International Marketplace is Waikiki's original shopping mall, built around an old banyan tree. Features an assortment of shops, galleries, clothing stores, jewelry stands, and restaurants. Open daily, 9 a.m.-10 p.m.

Kapiolani Park. Kalakaua Ave., between Kapahulu Ave. and Paki Ave., Waikiki. 100-acre public park, dedicated in 1877, to Queen Kapiolani, wife of King Kalakaua. The park is largely grassy, with palms, ironwoods and banyan trees. Also has tennis courts, a bandstand, the Honolulu Zoo, aquarium, and Kodak Hula Show. This is one of the most popular recreation areas in the Waikiki-Honolulu area, and the site of several local events.

Honolulu Zoo. 151 Kapahulu Ave., Honolulu; (808) 971-7171. Honolulu's largest and best-kept zoo. Features over 1,000 animals, including monkeys, elephants, giraffes and tigers, and a variety of birds. Also has a *Reptile House*, with some of Hawaii's only snakes; the *African Savannah*, featuring some 200 animals native to east Africa, all in natural settings; a *petting zoo*, and an *Elephant Encounter*, an educational program on elephants. The zoo is open daily, 9.00 a.m.-4.30 p.m.; "Elephant Encounter" at 11 a.m. Admission fee: $6.00 adults, $1.00 children 6-12.

Kodak Hula Show. At Kapiolani Park (near the bandstand), Waikiki. Popular outdoor show, featuring a live Hawaiian band—comprised of older Hawaiian women in traditional "mu'umu'us" and floppy hats—and a colorful, authentic "hula" dance performance with native Hawaiian women dancers in grass skirts. Open to the public free of charge; held on Tues., Wed., Thurs., 10-11.15 a.m.

Waikiki Aquarium. 2777 Kalakaua Ave., Waikiki; (808) 923-9741. Small aquarium with several excellent exhibits, including display tanks of reef sharks, turtles, Hawaiian monk seals, rays, octopi, a seahorse, giant clam, live coral, and deep-sea chambered nautilus. Also pool with simulated coral reef. Open 9-5 daily. Admission fee: $6.00 adults, $4.00 seniors, $2.50 children.

Natatorium War Memorial. Located on Kalakaua Ave., between the Waikiki Aquarium and Sans Souci State Recreation Area. Features a large stone facade, built in 1927 as a memorial to island men who fought in World War I. Also has a 100-meter salt-water pool.

Diamond Head Crater. At the southeast end of Waikiki, with the entrance to the crater located off Diamond Head Rd. (which goes off Kalakaua Ave.), near 18th Ave., from where a ½-mile trail leads to the inside of the crater. The crater is more than 100,000 years old, and it has as its highest point Leahi, at the southwest end of the crater rim, with an elevation of 760 feet; a 3/4-mile foot trail leads from the crater floor to Leahi, winding along a series of switchbacks and climbing some 200 steps through two tunnels, in the dark. There is a lookout at Leahi, with sweeping views of the Pacific Ocean. Open daily, 6 a.m.-6 p.m.

East Honolulu

Hanauma Bay Beach Park. Situated 1½ miles east of Maunalua Bay (7½ miles east of Waikiki), off Kalanianaole Hwy. (72); (808) 396-0933. Lovely, horseshoe-shaped aquamarine bay, abundant in a variety of marine life. This is in fact one of Oahu's most popular snorkeling spots, which also has at its north end, in the center of a reef, a protected, sandy-bottom area known as "Keyhole," ideal for swimming. Snack bar, fish food concession, snorkeling equipment rentals (available for $6.00 per set). The bay can also be reached on shuttle buses from Waikiki, for a fare of around 50 cents. Park hours: 7 a.m.-6 p.m. Free admission.

Scenic Overlook. Off Kalanianaole Hwy. (72), 3/4-mile east of Hanauma Bay. Offers views of Molokai on clear days, some 25 miles across the Kaiwi Channel.

Halona Cove/Blowhole. Located just off Kalanianaole Hwy. (72), at Halona Point, 1½-mile east of Hanauma Bay. Small, secluded cove, with a crescent-shaped sandy beach, and a blowhole, the Halona Blowhole, quite close to it. Also has views of nearby Sandy Beach, to the east.

Koko Crater. Located approximately 2 3/4 miles northeast of Hanauma Bay; reached by way of Kalanianaole Hwy. (72) northeastward from Hanauma Bay some 2 miles, then north on Kealahou Rd. ½ mile or so to a dirt road, which, in turn, heads off westward to the crater. The crater is horseshoe shaped, some 200 yards wide, and has as its highest point Pu'u Mai, at the southwest end of the crater rim, with an elevation of 1,204 feet. The crater is also home to the Koko Crater Botanical Gardens, presently in various stages of development. No facilities or visitor center. Open 9-4 daily.

Oahu 85

Sea Life Park. Off Kalanianaole Hwy. (72), 4½ miles northeast of Hanauma Bay, directly across from Makapu'u Beach Park, at Waimanalo; (808) 259-7933. 62-acre marine-life theme park, with an array of large pools and tanks displaying a variety of marine life, including whales, dolphins, sharks, Hawaiian monk seals, sea lions, turtles, penguins, and the world's only "wholphin"—the offspring of a killer whale and a bottlenose dolphin. Among the park's prominent exhibits are the huge *Hawaiian Reef Tank*, a 300,000-gallon aquarium with over 4,000 specimens; the *Rocky Shores*, an 11,000-gallon exhibit designed to recreate the surf- and wave-swept intertidal zone of Hawaii's shoreline; the *Hawaii Ocean Theater*, where bottlenose dolphins perform; and the *Whaler's Cove and Lagoon*, the *Sea Lion Feeding Pool*, *Seabird Sanctuary*, *Penguin Habitat*, *Turtle Lagoon*, and *Shark Gallery*. There is also a children's *touch pool* here, and the *Pacific Whaling Museum*, which boasts one of the largest collections of whaling artifacts and scrimshaw on the island. Live entertainment on weekends, as well as a sea lion show and a "Behind the Scenes" tour of the park. Also restaurant and gift shop on premises. Park hours: 9.30-5 daily (9 a.m.-10 p.m. on Fridays). Admission fee: $19.95 adults, $15.95 seniors, $9.95 children.

Pearl Harbor

USS Arizona Memorial. Arizona Place and Hwy. 90 west (off H1 Fwy.), Pearl Harbor; (808) 422-0561. One of the most-visited tourist attractions on the island, comprising a gracefully-arched, 184-foot-long white structure, built in 1962, directly over the battleship *USS Arizona*, which sank during the infamous Japanese attack on Pearl Harbor on December 7, 1941, entombing in its hull all 1,102 servicemen on board. There is also a *Visitor Center* at the memorial, with a theater showing a 20-minute documentary film on the attack, and a museum which has scale models of Pearl Harbor and the battleship before the attack. Snack bar, and bookstore. Visitor center hours: 7.30 a.m.-5 p.m. daily; program hours: 8 a.m.-3 p.m. (visitors are advised to arrive early for the program, as tickets to it sell out quickly, and there is usually a 1- to 3-hour wait; the program itself lasts approximately 1¼ hours).

USS Bowfin Submarine Museum and Park. Located adjacent to the USS Arizona Memorial Visitor Center, off Arizona Memorial Place and Hwy. 90, at Pearl Harbor; (808) 423-1341. 1,500-ton submarine, open to public tours. Self-guided tours—with pre-taped commentary piped through "sound sticks" —lead through various sections of the submarine, including the Captain's Room, officers' quarters, sleeping quarters, bunk room, mess-cum-kitchen, torpedo room, engine rooms, and a maneuvering room. Also museum on premises, with old photographs and exhibits depicting the history of submarines, and scale models and displays of torpedoes, instruments used to determine torpedo angles, depth charges, and control panels. On display, too, is a 12,000-pound, 34-foot-long C-3 Poseidon Missile with all its electronics, hydraulics and propulsion elements still intact. The museum and park are open daily, 8-5. Admission fee: $8.00 adults, $3.00 children, $6.00 seniors and military personnel; admission to the museum only is $4.00 adults, $2.00 children.

Moanalua Gardens. Situated off Mahiole St.—which goes off Puuloa Rd., which, in turn, goes off Moanalua Rd. (Hwy. 78)—approximately 3 miles east of Pearl Harbor; (808) 833-1944. Splendid 26-acre park, with huge monkey pod trees and a lily pond, located adjacent to the wooded Moanalua Valley. The park also has in it the *Royal House of Oahu*—the historic summer cottage of King Kamehameha V—and an old *Chinese meeting hall* with a carp pond, dating from the early 1900s. Good picnicking possibilities. Open Mon.-Fri., sunrise to sunset. Free admission.

Keaiwa Heiau State Recreation Area. Located at the end of Aeia Heights Dr.—which goes off Moanalua Rd. (Hwy. 78) near the Moanalua Gardens —2½ miles northeast of Pearl Harbor. Lush, hilltop park, abundant in ti plants, eucalyptus trees and Norfolk pines, with several good hiking trails winding through it. Also at the park is the ancient Keaiwa Heiau, 150 feet long and 100 feet wide. Views of Pearl Harbor, and camping possibilities. Open daily, 7 a.m.-7.45 p.m. Free admission.

Central Oahu

Waipahu Garden Cultural Park. 94-695 Waipahu St., Waipahu; (808) 677-0110. 50-acre theme park, established in 1992. Comprises an historic plantation village and outdoor museum, with 30 restored and replica 19th-century homes and buildings of various ethnic groups from the plantation era, including Hawaiian, Chinese, Portuguese, Puerto Rican, Japanese, Okinawan, Korean and Filipino, all with original, period furnishings. Highlights include the old Chinese Cookhouse, dating from 1909; the wood-frame Portuguese and Puerto Rico houses; the Filipino Dormitory, which once housed hen coops and warring rooster pens; the Hawaiian Hale, a thatched, wood-post structure on a coral and lava rock platform, dating from 1840-1876; and the Japanese Duplex, with its Shinto shrine and an 1800s, 15-foot-square Sumo Ring. Guided tours available. Open Mon.-Sat., 8-4. Admission: $5.00 adults, $3.00 children.

Wahiawa Botanical Garden. Located on California St., which goes off Kamehameha Hwy. (99), in Wahiawa; (808) 621-7321. 27-acre botanical garden, originally established in 1957 as a nursery and experimentation site for sugarcane. Now features a variety of flowers, plants and trees from around the world, including several types of spice trees, pandanus trees, bamboo, Australian Fern, Indian Mahogany, Travellers Tree, cinnamon, Hawaiian Fern, Hibiscus and other native Hawaiian plants. Open daily, 9-4. Free admission.

Tropical Lightning Museum. At the Schofield Barracks, just west of Wahiawa; located 3/4 mile from Foote Gate, at the corner of Waianae and Kolekole Aves. Displays are largely centered around the history of the Schofield Barracks. Also includes information and memorabilia from various conflicts, such as World War II and the Korean and Vietnam wars, and exhibits of old uniforms, field packs, rifles and machine guns, historic photographs, and even an exhibit of bunk inspections. Open Tues.-Sat., 10-4. Free admission.

Del Monte Pineapple Variety Garden. Located near the intersection of Hwys. 99 and 80, 1½ miles north of Wahiawa. Variety of pineapple plants on display, from the Bahamas, South Africa, Samoa, Malaya, the Philippines and Brazil. Also features an exhibit centered around the history of pineapple production in Hawaii. Open daily.

Dole Plantation. 64-1550 Kamehameha Hwy. (99), Wahiawa; (808) 621-8408. Large, 10,000-square-foot tourist-alluring gift shop, situated amid pineapple fields. Offers a variety of fresh fruit and fruit juices, and island souvenirs. There is also a variety garden at the plantation, with sample pineapple plants from around the world, together with a vegetable garden specializing in growing record-size plants. Also at the plantation is the world's largest maze, built from 11,400 Hawaiian plants, including hibiscus, heliconia and plumeria, and with a pineapple-shaped garden at its center. The maze encompasses approximately 100,000 square feet, and features a 1.7-mile-long path. Admission to the maze is $4.50 adults, and $2.50 children. Open daily, 9-5.30.

Oahu 87

North Shore

Liliuokalani Church. Located on Kamehameha Hwy. (83), near the corner of Emerson Rd., in Haleiwa. Steepled church, with walls of coral and wood, originally built in 1832 and rebuilt in 1961. The church has in it a century-old clock that shows not only the time, day of the week and month, but also the phase of the moon. Open daily.

Waimea Bay. Situated approximately 3 miles northeast of Haleiwa; reached by way of Kamehemeha Hwy. (83). Picture-perfect aquamarine bay, with a beautiful, crescent-shaped white-sand beach. Also premier surfing spot, and site of several surfing contests, including the prestigious, annual Quicksilver/ Eddie Aikau Memorial Big Wave Classic, which is held only when waves crest at over 20 feet.

Waimea Falls Park. 59-864 Kamehameha Hwy. (83), Haleiwa; (808) 638-8511. 1,800-acre park, located across the highway from the Waimea Bay Beach Park, in the ancient Waimea Valley. Features several historical sites—including remnants of *heiaus* and a fishing shrine—and a botanical garden with nearly 6,000 species of tropical flora from around the world, including more than 400 species of rare and endangered Hawaiian and South Pacific plants. Also several colorful events, such as cliff diving at the 45-foot-high Waimea Falls, *hula* performances, and an assortment of traditional Hawaiian sports and games, among them *o'o ihe*, the age-old sport of spear throwing. There are, besides, some good swimming possibilities in the natural pools here, and hiking trails winding through the Waimea Valley. Narrated tram tours, as well as guided walks of park available. Restaurant, snack bar and gift shops on premises. Open daily 10-5.30; admission fee: $19.95 adults, $9.95 children (ages 6-12).

Pu'uomahuka Heiau State Monument. Situated on Pupukea Rd., which goes off Kamehameha Hwy. (83), eastward, directly across from Pupukea Beach —which lies approximately 1 mile north of Waimea Bay. The Pu'uomahuka Heiau, meaning "Hill of Escape," is the largest heiau on Oahu, 575 feet long and 170 feet wide, believed to have been built by the menehune, Hawaii's mysterious little people. The heiau is situated at an elevation of around 300 feet, overlooking Waimea Bay and the North Shore, and comprises three large terraces, each defined by a low stone wall along its perimeter. There is also an ancient paved trail that journeys around the heiau. Open to the public 7 a.m.-7 p.m.

Banzai Pipeline. At Ehukai Beach Park, just to the southwest of Sunset Beach, off Kamehameha Hwy. (83). The "Banzai Pipeline" is one of Hawaii's most famous waves, with a 200-yard break and an almost-perfect tube, rising to heights of 20 to 30 feet. Site of several surfing competitions, including the annual Pipeline Masters Surfing Championships. Best viewed during the winter months.

Windward Coast

Kahuku Sugar Mill. Located on Kamehameha Hwy. (83), ½ mile north of mile marker 16 (3 miles north Laie), at Kahuku; (808) 293-8747. Housed in the old mill building, dating from 1890, which now also houses the Kahuku Sugar Mill Shopping Center, with some gift shops and a restaurant. There are self-guided tours of the old mill, which has its 19th-century mill machinery on display, all brightly painted and labeled. Open 8-5 Mon.-Sat.; tour cost: $1.00.

Hawaii Mormon Temple. 55-645 Naniloa Loop (off Kamehemeha Hwy., 83), Laie; (808) 293-9297. Replica of the Mormon Temple in Salt Lake City, built in 1919, from volcanic rock and concrete. Landscaped grounds, with palms and a series of pools. The church has films and information on the temple and highlights of the original Mormon missionaries in Hawaii. Only church members are allowed inside the church. Open 9-8 daily.

Polynesian Cultural Center. Kamehameha Hwy. (83), at mile marker 19, in Laie; (808) 293-3333/(800) 367-7060. One of the most popular island attractions, comprising a 42-acre complex with 7 authentically recreated Polynesian villages—connected by lagoons—representing the South Pacific cultures of Samoa, New Zealand, Tahiti, Fiji, the Marquesas, Tonga and old Hawaii. The villages feature arts and crafts and demonstrations in poi pounding, coconut husking and making tapa cloth from tree bark, among other activities. Also Polynesian song and dance extravaganzas, including the long-running "Pageant of the Long Canoes" and "This is Polynesia," and Hawaiian luau dinners and lavish buffets. The center is open Mon.-Sat., 12.30-6 p.m. Admission fee: $27.00 adults, $16.00 children; admission and buffet dinner: $47.00 adults, $30.00 children; admission and luau with entertainment: $64.00 adults, $43.00 children.

Sacred Falls State Park. Off Kamehameha Hwy. (83), 4 3/4 miles north of Crouching Lion Inn. Idyllic, 1,374-acre nature preserve, with 80-foot-high waterfall. The waterfall is located deep inside the park, reached by way of a 2-mile foot trail that leads from the parking area near the park entrance, passing through some lush vegetation, to the falls. There is a large natural pool at the foot of the falls, ideal for swimming.

Kauhi'imakaokalani (Crouching Lion). Situated approximately 13 miles north of Kaneohe, off Kamehameha Hwy. (83), near mile marker 27. Kauhi'imakaokalani—or "Crouching Lion"—is the mountain ridge which rises, on the inland side of the highway, directly behind the Crouching Lion Inn. It vaguely resembles a crouching lion.

Kualoa Regional Park. Off Kamehameha Hwy. (836), at Kualoa Point, just over 5 miles north of the intersection of Kahekili Hwy. (83). 150-acre public park, with a narrow beach with picnic tables and a lifeguard. The park is largely grassy, dotted with palm trees. Park hours: 7 a.m.-8 p.m.

Mokoli'i Island (Chinaman's Hat). Located just offshore from Kualoa Regional Park, at Kualoa. The island is named for its distinctive shape, resembling a traditional Chinese peasant hat.

He'eia State Park. Off Kamehameha Hwy. (836), 1½ miles north of the intersection of Haiku Rd. and the Windward Mall in Kaneohe. This is a largely grassy park, situated at Kealohi Point, overlooking Kaneohe Bay and the ancient, 88-acre He'eia Fishpond. Also offers good views of Moku o Loe (Coconut Island).

Byodo-In Temple. Situated in the Valley of the Temples, at 47-200 Kahekili Hwy. (83)—approximately 2½ miles north of the intersection of Likelike Hwy. (63)—in Kaneohe; (808) 239-8811. Splendid replica of a 900-year-old Buddhist temple in Kyoto, Japan, built in 1968. Features a 3-ton ceremonial brass bell and a 9-foot gold-and-lacquer Buddha, seated on a carved lotus. Also landscaped Japanese gardens, with 2-acre reflecting pond with swans, ducks and carp. Gift shop and tea house on premises. Open daily.

Ho'omaluhia Botanical Garden. Situated in Kaneohe, at the end of Luluku Rd., which goes off Kamehameha Hwy. (83), just south of Likelike Hwy. (63); (808) 235-6636. Lush, 400-acre garden, featuring plants and trees from various parts of the world, including the Philippines, Malaysia, the Americas, Africa, Australia, India, Sri Lanka and Hawaii. The garden also has several good hiking and horseback riding trails, and a 32-acre lake. Visitor center on premises, with maps and information for garden tours and other scheduled programs. Open daily, 9-4; guided nature walks on weekends. Free admission.

Ulupo Heiau State Historical Site. Located just inland from the Kailua and Lanikai beaches, in Kailua; reached by way of Pali Hwy. (61) east from the intersection of Kalanianaole Hwy. (72) a little way, then north on Ulupo St. a block or so, and right—east—onto Manu Aloha St., and, again, right—or south

Oahu 89

—on Manu O'o St. which leads to the YMCA and on to the *heiau*. The *heiau* is 180 feet long and 140 feet wide, believed to have been built by the *menehune*, Hawaii's legendary little people. There are also good views from the *heiau*, of the Kawainui Swamp just to the west.

Waianae Coast

Kuilioloa Heiau. Located at Kane'ilio Point, at the southwest end of Pokai Bay Beach, off Farrington Hwy. (93), Waianae. Historic *heiau*, surrounded on three sides by the ocean. The *heiau* is 150 feet long and 35 feet wide, featuring three platforms, all descending to Kane'ilio Point. It was once also a place of refuge.

Kaneaki Heiau. Located in the Mauna Olu Estates; reached by way of Makaha Valley Rd.—which goes northeastward off Farrington Hwy. (93)—approximately 1 3/4 miles, then east on Maunaolu St., ½ mile, to Alahele St. which leads northeastward, another ½ mile, to the *heiau*. This is one of the best preserved *heiaus* on Oahu, 150 feet long and 75 feet wide, comprising an altar surrounded by "tikis"—idols—and two thatched houses—Halemana, the "house of spiritual power," and Halepahu, the "drum house." The *heiau* was originally built between 1470 and 1640, and enlarged and modified three times, the last in the late 1700s, converting it into a war temple. Lush valley setting, amid *ti* plants and groves of Palm, guava and banana trees. Picnicking possibilities. The heiau is open to the public 10-2, Tues.-Sun.; visitors must sign in at the gate.

Kaena Point Natural Area Preserve. Located at the end of Farrington Hwy. (93), in the northwest corner of the island, approximately 5½ miles north of Makaha. Remote natural preserve, with a long, golden-sand beach, overlooking Kaena Point, the westernmost point on the island. There is a 2-mile trail that journeys along a flat, arid stretch, from the reserve to Kaena Point. The reserve is also the site of the historic Oahu Land & Railway Company railroad, which operated from here from 1895 to 1947. The reserve is open to the public.

BEACHES

Oahu has some of the loveliest beaches in the Pacific, sandy, sunny, and in delightful settings, especially along the island's North Shore and at Waikiki. All beaches are public beaches; however, nude bathing at Hawaii's public beaches is prohibited under state law—although some of the beaches continue to be frequented by nudists. Also, a word of caution: several of the beaches on the island are subject to strong under-currents or rip tides, especially in the winter and spring months, making swimming at these beaches, at such times, inadvisable, frequently dangerous; due caution must therefore be exercised at all times when approaching the ocean.

Honolulu

Ala Moana Beach Park. Off Ala Moana Blvd., directly across from the Ala Moana Shopping Center. Popular, 77-acre beach park, with wide, mile-long sandy beach. Offers safe swimming conditions, due to protective reef; also picnicking and jogging possibilities, and tennis courts, softball field, snack bar, restrooms and showers, and on-duty lifeguard.

Aina Moana Beach Park (Magic Island). Located at the east end of Ala Moana Beach Park, off Ala Moana Park Dr., which goes off Ala Moana

Blvd. The "island" is in fact a 36-acre man-made peninsula, bordering the Ala Wai Harbor and canal. It comprises a large, grassy park area with shade trees, and a lagoon and crescent-shaped sandy beach at the tip of the peninsula. Offers safe swimming conditions, and picnic tables, showers and restrooms, and a lifeguard. The beach park is open 7.45 a.m.-7 p.m. daily.

Waikiki

Duke Kahanamoku Beach. Located off Kalia Rd., directly in front of the Hilton Hawaiian Village. Named in honor of Duke Kahanamoku, champion surfer and swimmer, who won the gold medal in the 100-meter freestyle at the 1912 Olympics. This is the westernmost beach at Waikiki, broad, palm-fringed, and with a gently-sloping sandy bottom. Offers generally safe swimming conditions year-round, due to a protective pier and breakwater. Beach facilities include a lifeguard, and showers.

Fort DeRussy Beach Park. Located at Fort DeRussy, off Kalia Rd. This is the widest section of the white-sand Waikiki Beach—nearly 100 yards wide—bordered by a large, grassy area with palm trees. Good swimming possibilities year-round. Lifeguard, picnic tables, showers and restrooms.

Gray's Beach. Situated off Kalia Rd., in front of Halekulani Hotel, with a public access leading from Kalia Rd., between the Outrigger Reef and Halekulani hotels, to the beach. The beach is small, sandy, and quite popular with long-distance swimmers. No facilities.

Royal Moana Beach. Situated directly in front of the Royal Hawaiian and Sheraton Moana Surfrider hotels, in the heart of Waikiki, off Kalakaua Ave., and frequently crowded. Offers a gently-sloping sandy bottom, and two popular surf breaks just offshore, *Queen's Surf* and *Canoe's Surf*. Excellent swimming, surfing and sailing possibilities, year-round.

Waikiki Beach Center. Located across from the Hyatt Regency Waikiki hotel, near the Waikiki-Honolulu Police Station, off Kalakaua Ave. White-sand beach section, with good swimming and surfing possibilities. Facilities here include a lifeguard station, surfboard rental concession, and showers and restrooms.

Kuhio Beach Park. Kalakaua Ave., between Liliuokalani Ave. and Kapahulu Ave. This is one of Waikiki's finest beach areas, which has in it the *Kapahulu Groin*, a storm drain extending southwestward from Kapahulu Avenue into the ocean, quite popular with boogie-boarders. There is also a retaining stone wall here, that runs northwestward from the storm drain, parallel to the shoreline, enclosing in it two natural pools, protected from the open ocean and excellent for swimming. Beach facilities include a lifeguard, and showers.

Kapiolani Beach Park. Located between Kuhio Beach and the Sans Souci Recreation Area, off Kalakaua Ave. Kapiolani is a well-liked sandy beach, adjoining to the southeast of the Kuhio Beach Park, and bordered by a large, palm-fringed grassy area with picnic tables. At its western end, nearer to the Kapahulu Groin and Kuhio Beach, the beach is quite narrow, bordered by patches of coral and lava rock; but it quickly fans out, near the center, into a wide section known as the *Queen's Surf Beach*, quite popular with the gay community. Sandy bottom; excellent for swimming. Facilities include a lifeguard, and showers and restrooms.

Sans Souci State Recreation Area. Off Kalakaua Ave., at the New Otani Kaimana Beach Hotel. Small, sandy beach area, and the easternmost and least crowded of the beaches at Waikiki. Features a gently-sloping sandy bottom, ideal for swimming and snorkeling. Lifeguard, showers, and portable toilets.

Kuilei Cliffs Beach Park. Located 3/4 mile east of Kapiolani Park, off Diamond Head Rd.; reached by way of a paved pathway that dashes off from the first of three lookouts here, at the foot of Diamond Head, leading down to the beach. The beach is long, narrow, and bordered by a coral reef, generally not suitable for swimming. There is a shower at the beach.

East Honolulu

Maunalua Bay Beach Park. Located along Kalanianaole Hwy. (72), approximately 5 miles east of Diamond Head. The Maunalua Beach Park is one of a series of beaches strung along Maunalua Bay, protected from the ocean by a reef that extends some 4 miles, just offshore, along the length of the bay. The beach had good jet skiing, windsurfing, para-sailing, boating and fishing possibilities. Beach facilities include a boat ramp and showers and restrooms.

Hanauma Bay Beach Park. 7½ miles east of Waikiki (1½ miles east of Maunalua Bay), reached on Kalanianaole Hwy. (72). This picturesque, horseshoe-shaped aquamarine bay, which has an established underwater marine life reserve, is one of the best and most popular snorkeling spots on the island. The bay also has, near its north end, in the center of a reef that protects it from the open ocean, a sandy-bottom area known as "Keyhole," ideal for swimming. Beach park facilities include a lifeguard station, picnic area, and showers and restrooms; also snorkeling equipment rentals, and food concession. Park hours: 7 a.m.-6 p.m.

Halona Cove. Off Kalanianaole Hwy. (72), at Halona Point, 1½ miles east of Hanauma Bay; accessed by way of a trail that leads from the west side of the parking lot, down to the beach. The beach is small, crescent shaped, and located inside a cove. Swimming, however, is inadvisable, due to the strong under-currents. There is also a blowhole here, just to the east of the beach, and good views of Sandy Beach to the northeast. No facilities.

Sandy Beach Park. Located off Kalanianaole Hwy. (72), ¼ mile northeast of Halona Cove (1 3/4 miles northeast of Hanauma Bay). This is one of the most popular bodysurfing spots on the island, and the site of several bodysurfing contests. The beach itself is long and wide, bordering a large grassy area that is ideally suited to kite-flying and picnicking. Swimming, however, is not encouraged due to the dangerous rip tides. Beach facilities include lifeguards, showers and restrooms.

Makapu'u Beach Park. 2½ miles northeast of Sandy Beach (4¼ miles northeast of Hanauma Bay), off Kalanianaole Hwy. (72). Crescent-shaped sandy beach, bordered by coral and backed by low sand dunes, situated between two rocky points below the Makapu'u Lighthouse. Makapu'u Beach is also quite popular with bodysurfers, although swimming is not recommended due to the strong under-currents. Lifeguard station, picnic tables, showers and restrooms.

North Shore

Mokuleia Beach Park. Located off Farrington Hwy. (930), 4½ miles west of Waialua. 12-acre beach park, with a long, narrow stretch of beach, backed by small dunes covered with vegetation. The beach attracts primarily windsurfers and fishermen. Swimming is not advised, due to choppy waters and strong currents and the coral. The park also includes a large grassy area, with camping facilities, picnic tables, showers and restrooms.

Haleiwa Ali'i Beach Park. Off Haleiwa Rd., ¼ mile west of the inter-section of Kamehameha Hwy. (83), in Haleiwa. Broad, sandy beach, bordered by a coral reef, and notable as one of the premier surfing spots where several surfing contests are held during the winter months. Beach facilities include a lifeguard station, picnic tables, restrooms, and showers. Also ample parking.

Kaiaka State Recreation Area. Located ½ mile west of Haleiwa Ali'i Beach Park, along Haleiwa Rd. (which goes off Kamehameha Hwy.), in Haleiwa. The park is situated along the northeast end of Kaiaka Bay, at Kaiaka Point. It has a small, sandy, coral beach, backing onto a large lawn area with a handful of ironwood trees. Swimming is not advisable, due to the strong ocean currents. There are, however, some camping possibilities here, and picnic tables and restrooms.

Haleiwa Beach Park. Situated off Kamehameha Hwy. (83), approximately 1½ miles northeast of mile marker 0, just north of the Anahulu Stream Bridge. 13-acre beach park, with a thin, palm-fringed beach. Offers swimming, surfing and fishing possibilities. Also baseball and basketball facilities, and showers and restrooms.

Laniakea Beach. Located roughly 2 miles northeast of Haleiwa Beach Park, off Kamehameha Hwy. (83). Roadside beach, and a popular surfing spot in the winter months. The beach is fairly long, and bordered by a coral reef. Swimming is not encouraged due to the adverse ocean conditions. No facilities; parking alongside the highway.

Chun's Reef. Off Kamehameha Hwy. (83); ½ mile northeast of Laniakea Beach (2¼ miles northeast of Haleiwa Beach Park). Another popular North Shore surfing beach—especially in the winter months—bordered by coral. Swimming is not recommended due to the strong under-currents. No facilities; roadside parking.

Waimea Bay Beach Park. Kamehameha Hwy. (83), 4 miles northeast of Haleiwa Beach Park. Well-liked beach park, with a picturesque, crescent-shaped sandy beach. This is also one of the island's premier surfing spots, and the site of several surfing competitions, including the Quicksilver/Eddie Aikau Memorial Big Wave Classic, which is held only when waves reach heights of 20 feet or more. Swimming is not encouraged during the winter months. Facilities include a lifeguard station, picnic tables, and showers and restrooms.

Pupukea Beach Park. Off Kamehameha Hwy. (83), 1 mile northeast of Waimea Bay Beach Park (5 miles northeast of Haleiwa Beach Park). There are two places of coastal access at the beach park: a small, sandy beach at the western end of the park, surrounded by lava rock, coral and tidepools, known as *Three Tables*, for the three rocky ledges rising from the water just offshore; and *Shark's Cove*, at the northeastern end of the park, featuring several tidepools. Both *Shark's Cove* and the *Three Tables* offer good snorkeling and diving possibilities in the summer months; during winter, however, the ocean conditions here are unsuitable for any water sport. Park facilities include basketball courts, a children's play area, camping facilities, showers, and restrooms.

Ehukai Beach Park. Situated along Kamehameha Hwy. (83), 1½ miles northeast of Pupukea Beach Park, directly across from the Sunset Elementary School, with parking available along Ke Nui Rd., which runs parallel to the highway, on the ocean side. Ehukai is a long, wide beach, backed by ironwood trees and a grassy area directly above. It is also one of the most famous surfing spots in the islands, home to the world-renowned "Banzai Pipeline," the site of several international surfing competitions. Swimming is not recommended here, due to the dangerous under-currents. On-duty lifeguard, picnic tables, showers and restroom facilities.

Sunset Beach Park. Situated off Kamehameha Hwy. (83), 3/4 mile northeast of Ehukai Beach Park. Broad, white-sand beach, lined with palm trees and bordered by coral. This is also one of Hawaii's famous surfing beaches, where several surfing contests are held each year. Again, swimming is not encouraged during the winter months, due to the high surf and strong currents. The beach, however, also has some windsurfing possibilities, along its east end, just off Sunset Point. Beach facilities include a lifeguard, and portable toilets.

Kuilima Cove. Located at the Turtle Bay Hilton and Country Club, off Kamehameha Hwy. (83), 4 miles northeast of Sunset Beach Park. Small, crescent-shaped sandy beach, situated in a cove, between two lava rock outcroppings. Features a protective reef, and abundant coral, making this an especially good place for snorkeling; also safe swimming conditions. Canoe and kayak rentals, and showers and restroom facilities. Parking fee.

Windward Coast

Malaekahana Bay State Recreation Area. Situated along Kamehameha Hwy. (83), just south of Kahuku. Popular family beach park, situated between Kalanai Point and Makahoa Point, along Malaekahana Bay. The beach is long, narrow, and bordered by clusters of coral and lined with hala and ironwood trees. Offers generally safe swimming conditions, and views Moku Auia—or Goat Island—just offshore from Kalanai Point, at the south end of the bay. Also some camping possibilities, and picnic tables, barbecue pits, showers and restrooms.

Pounder's Beach. Off Kamehameha Hwy. (83), between mile markers 19 and 20, ½ mile south of Laie. Crescent-shaped sandy beach, bordering a grassy area with hala and ironwood trees. The beach is named for its pounding shorebreak, quite attractive to bodysurfers. The beach is also frequented by fishermen. Swimming is inadvisable due to the dangerous under-currents. No beach facilities.

Hau'ula Beach Park. Located at Hau'ula, along Kamehameha Hwy. (83), near mile marker 21, approximately 2 miles south of Laie. Roadside beach, long, narrow, and lined with ironwood and palm trees. Features a protective coral reef, with safe swimming and snorkeling. Beach facilities include picnic tables, showers and restrooms.

Punalu'u Beach Park. Located off Kamehameha Hwy. (83), some 3 miles south of Hau'ula. Long, narrow roadside beach, bordered by a coral reef. Safe for swimming and snorkeling. Facilities include picnic tables, showers and restrooms.

Kahana Bay Beach Park. Situated along Kahana Bay, off Kamehameha Hwy. (83), roughly 1 3/4 miles south of Punalu'u Beach (some 7 miles south of Laie). 8-acre beach park, with a beautiful, crescent-shaped white-sand beach, lined with ironwood trees, quite popular with vacationing families. Offers good, safe swimming, as well as some fishing possibilities. Also views of the ancient Huila Fishpond to the southeast. There is a boat ramp at the north end of the beach, and picnic tables and restroom facilities.

Swanzy Beach Park. Off Kamehameha Hwy. (83), approximately a mile southeast of Kahana Bay. This is a multi-use, rocky shoreline park, which, however, has no beach as such. Park facilities include a baseball diamond, basketball courts, children's play area, picnic tables, showers and restrooms.

Ka'a'awa Beach Park. Off Kamehameha Hwy. (83), 1 mile south of Swanzy Beach Park (2 miles southeast of Kahana Bay), in Ka'a'awa. Small, narrow roadside beach, with a protective coral reef just offshore, offering generally safe swimming and snorkeling. Beach facilities include picnic tables, showers and a restroom.

Kalaeolio Beach Park. Situated along Kamehameha Hwy. (83), on the north side of Ka'a'awa Stream, ¼ mile south of Ka'a'awa Beach Park. Small, sandy beach, backed by ironwood trees. Offers some swimming and snorkeling possibilities in calm seas. Also picnic tables. No other beach facilities.

Kanenelu Beach. Situated a mile south of Kalaeolio Beach Park (2 miles south of Ka'a'awa), off Kamehameha Hwy. (83). Thin, long, roadside beach, attracting primarily fishermen, surfers and beachcombers. Some swimming possibilities. No facilities.

Kualoa Regional Park. Located along Kamehameha Hwy. (83), at Kualoa

(Apua) Point, 1½ miles south of Kanenelu Beach (approximately 3½ miles north of the town of Waiahole). Narrow, coral-lined beach, generally safe for swimming. The beach is part of a 150-acre park, which also includes a large lawn area dotted with palms. Views of Kaneohe Bay and Chinaman's Hat. On-duty lifeguard, picnic tables, restrooms and showers. Open 7 a.m.-7 p.m.

Kailua Beach Park. Located at the end of Kailua Rd. (which is really an extension of Pali Hwy., 61), in Kailua; reached by way of Kailua Rd. east to the intersection of South Kalaheo Ave., then south on South Kalaheo Ave., approximately 3/4 mile, and east, again, on Kailua Rd., which leads more or less directly to the beach parking lot. This is of course one of the most beautiful white-sand beaches on Oahu, long, wide, backed by low sand dunes, and with a gently-sloping sandy bottom and crystal-clear aquamarine water. Swimming is generally safe here year-round, making it ideally suited for children. Also windsurfing and ocean kayaking. Facilities include a boat ramp at the southern end of the beach, and picnic tables, showers and restrooms.

Lanikai Beach. Situated just to the south of Kailua Beach, and accessed from Mokulua Drive, which goes off the one-way A'alapapa Drive. Lanikai is a lovely, uncrowded white-sand beach, stretching nearly a mile, and lined with beachfront homes. It offers good, safe swimming conditions year-round. No facilities; limited parking.

Bellows Field Beach Park. Situated off Kalanianaole Hwy. (72), approximately 1½ miles north of Waimanalo Beach. 46-acre beach park, with a long, sandy beach, situated at Bellows Air Force Station. The beach offers generally safe swimming conditions, some camping on weekends, and fishing and surfing. Picnic tables, showers, restrooms. The park is open to the public on weekends.

Waimanalo Bay State Recreation Area. Off Kalanianaole Hwy. (72), 1¼ miles north of Waimanalo Beach. The park has in it a mile-long white-sand beach, bordered by a lawn area with shade trees, quite popular with area residents. Good surfing and bodysurfing possibilities; some swimming. Beach facilities include picnic tables, showers and restrooms.

Waimanalo Beach Park. Situated along Waimanalo Bay, off Kalanianaole Hwy. (72), 2¼ miles south of Kailua. Long, white-sand beach, curving around Waimanalo Bay, backed by shallow sand dunes and ironwood trees. Offers good, safe swimming year-round; also some camping possibilities, and a baseball field, basketball courts, picnic tables, showers and restrooms.

Kaiona Beach Park. Located off Kalanianaole Hwy. (72), 3/4 mile south of Waimanalo Beach. The beach is narrow, rocky, and protected by an outer reef and backed by a grassy area with picnic tables, showers and restrooms. Offers some swimming and snorkeling possibilities.

Kaupo Beach Park. Situated off Kalanianaole Hwy. (72), 2¼ miles south of Waimanalo Beach (¼ mile north of Sea Life Park). Small, sandy beach, bordered by a coral reef. The beach attracts primarily surfers and fishermen. Some swimming possibilities. No facilities.

Waianae Coast

(Note: Beaches on the Waianae—leeward—Coast, although quite beautiful and idyllic, can often be less inviting and even unsafe, due to the presence of derelicts and indigents, and the prevailing racial tensions. Visitors primarily should be cautious when approaching these beaches. Among the beaches with the most problems are Barbers Point, Kahe Point, Lualualei and Makua.)

Ewa Beach Park. Located approximately 6½ miles southwest of Waipahu, at the end of Fort Weaver Rd., which goes off the H1 Fwy., southward. The beach park has in it a broad, sandy beach with a coral reef, frequented primarily by bodysurfers and fishermen, and a large, grassy area with baseball and

Oahu 95

basketball facilities, picnic tables, children's play area, and restrooms and showers. Also offers views of Honolulu and Diamond Head.

Barbers Point Beach Park. Situated some 5 miles west of Waipahu, at Barbers Point; reached by way of H1 Fwy. west to Kalaeloa Blvd., then south on Kalaeloa Blvd. 2½ miles, and southwestward on Olai St. another 3/4 mile to the beach park. Barbers Point Beach is a thin, coral-lined beach, with choppy waters, named for a pioneer trader, Captain Henry Barber, who ran aground here in 1796. The beach has some picnic tables and restrooms facilities. Also views of Diamond Head.

Kahe Point Beach Park. Off Farrington Hwy. (93), 4 miles north of mile marker on H1 Fwy. (or 3 miles north of the beginning of Hwy. 93), on the south side of the Hawaiian Electric plant. The beach park is situated on low cliffs, and bordered by coral and rocks. It attracts primarily fishermen. Swimming is not recommended due to adverse ocean conditions. Park facilities include a pavilion, and picnic tables.

Manner's Beach. Off Farrington Hwy. (93), ¼ mile northwest of the Hawaiian Electric plant, near Nanakuli. Small strand of golden sand, situated between Kahe Point and Pili O Kahe Point, backed by kiawe trees and sand dunes, quite attractive to surfers and beachcombers. Offers some camping possibilities; also restrooms.

Nanakuli Beach Park. Situated along Farrington Hwy. (93), at Nanakuli Ave., Nanakuli. The beach park comprises two crescent-shaped coves with golden sand, separated by low cliffs and coral, with good swimming and snorkeling possibilities in the summer months, when the ocean is relatively calm; swimming, however, is not advised in winter due to the adverse conditions. The beach has a lifeguard station, camping facilities, showers and restrooms; also community center, ball field, and a children's play area.

Ulehawa Beach Park #1. Off Farrington Hwy. (93), just over a mile north of Nanakuli Beach Park, Nanakuli. Ulehawa is a long, narrow beach, situated alongside the Ulehawa Stream. It is fronted by a coral reef, with a few sandy areas, and backed by shallow sand dunes, lined with palm trees and kiawe. Attracts primarily fishermen. Swimming is not recommended, due to the strong currents and unfavorable ocean conditions. There is a restroom at the beach.

Ulehawa Beach Park #2. Located along Farrington Hwy. (93), 2 miles northwest of Ulehawa Beach Park #1, just north of Maili Point. This is a sandy beach, interspersed with abundant coral, and backed by low sand dunes. Swimming is generally not advised during the winter months; however, there is a small, protected area here, enclosed by coral, ideal for children to swim in, in calm weather. The beach also has some surfing possibilities. Facilities include picnic tables and a restroom.

Maili Beach Park. Off Farrington Hwy. (93), ½ mile north of Ulehawa Beach Park #2, in Maili. Mile-long beach; comprises pockets of sand and coral, and a broad lawn area with picnic tables and children's play equipment. Offers some swimming possibilities in the summer months, and surfing. Beach facilities include a lifeguard, and showers and restrooms.

Lualualei Beach Park. Situated a mile north of Maili Beach Park, off Farrington Hwy. (93), in Waianae. Long, sandy beach, randomly punctuated with coral, and somewhat less attractive due to the presence of derelicts and unfriendly locals. The beach is backed by low sand dunes. Restroom facilities.

Pokai Bay Beach Park. Located on Pokai Bay St., west of Waianae Valley Rd., off Farrington Hwy., in Waianae. Makai is a crescent-shaped sandy beach, protected from the open ocean by breakwaters. It is in fact one of the safest swimming beaches on the Waianae Coast. The beach park also has a large, grassy area, and picnic tables, on-duty lifeguard, showers and restrooms.

Mauna Lahilahi Beach Park. Situated along Farrington Hwy. (93), across from the intersection of Makaha Valley Rd., some 2 miles northwest of Waianae

Valley Rd., in Makaha. Roadside sandy beach, bordered by coral. Swimming is not advised during the winter months, due to the high seas and strong undercurrents. Beach facilities include picnic tables, showers and restrooms.

Papaoneone Beach. Off Farrington Hwy. (93), 2½ miles northwest of the intersection of Waianae Valley Rd. ½ mile north of Mauna Lahilahi Beach), with a beach access between Lahilahi and Moua Rds. This is a sandy, quarter-mile-long beach, situated in a lovely cove. It offers some swimming and surfing possibilities. No beach facilities.

Makaha Beach Park. Off Farrington Hwy. (93), 1½ miles northwest of the intersection of Makaha Valley Rd., Makaha. Long, wide, golden-sand beach, bordered by coral. This is also a very popular surfing spot, with 25- to 30-foot-high waves in winter, and the site of several surfing contests each year, including Buffalo's Big Board Surfing Classic. Swimming possibilities in the summer months. On-duty lifeguard, restrooms and showers.

Kea'au Beach Park. Located on Farrington Hwy. (93), approximately a mile northwest of Makaha. Shoreline park, with a large, grassy area with picnic tables under kiawe trees. There is, however, no beach here, and swimming, too, is not advised due to the unfavorable ocean conditions. Offers some camping possibilities, and showers and restrooms.

Makua Beach. Off Farrington Hwy. (93), 3 miles north of Makaha. Makua is a broad, sandy beach, which was once used as a landing for canoes. It is now frequented primarily by fishermen, and long-term campers, making it somewhat less attractive to visitors. No beach facilities.

Kaena Point Natural Area Preserve. Located at the end of Farrington Hwy. (93), some 5 miles northwest of Makaha. There is a long, golden-sand beach at the reserve, backed by small sand dunes. Offers some bodysurfing possibilities, although coral and the strong ocean currents often create adverse conditions. Views of Kaena Point. Beach park facilities include showers and restrooms.

CAMPGROUNDS

State Park Campgrounds

(Camping at state campgrounds is permitted Fri.-Tues. only. For camping permits and information on the campgrounds, contact the *Division of State Parks*, 1151 Punchbowl St., Room 310, Honolulu, HI 96813; 808-587-0300.)

Keaiwa Heiau State Recreation Area. Located at the end of Aeia Heights Dr.—which goes off Moanalua Rd. (Hwy. 78) near the Moanalua Gardens—2½ miles northeast of Pearl Harbor. Offers hilltop campsites, quite popular with island families. Facilities include picnic tables, restrooms and showers. Also nearby wilderness, abundant in ti plants, Norfolk pines and eucalyptus, with several good hiking trails winding through it.

Kahana Bay Beach Park. Situated along Kahana Bay, off Kamehameha Hwy. (83), approximately 7 miles south of Laie, on the island's Windward Coast. 8-acre park, with a white-sand beach lined with ironwood trees. Campsites located on beach, with picnic tables and restroom facilities. Also swimming and fishing possibilities, and views of the ancient Huila Fishpond to the southeast.

Malaekahana Bay State Recreation Area. Located on the ocean side of Kamehameha Hwy. (83), just south of Kahuku, on the Windward Coast. Popular family beach park, situated along Malaekahana Bay, with campsites situated amid groves of ironwood and hala trees directly above the beach. Some

Oahu

swimming possibilities, and views of Moku Auia—or Goat Island—just offshore. Park facilities include picnic tables, barbecue pits, and showers and restrooms.

County Park Campgrounds

(Camping at county park campgrounds is permitted Fri.-Tues. only. For camping permits and information on the campgrounds, contact the *Department of Parks & Recreation*, Honolulu Municipal Building, 650 South King St., Honolulu, HI 96813; 808-523-4525.)

Makapu'u Beach Park. Situated at the southeast corner of the island, some 4¼ miles northeast of Hanauma Bay (11 3/4 miles east of Waikiki), off Kalanianaole Hwy. (72). The park has a sandy beach with campsites, nestled amid low cliffs. Good bodysurfing possibilities. Lifeguard station, picnic tables, showers and restrooms.

Waimanalo Beach Park. Off Kalanianaole Hwy. (72), 2¼ miles south of Kailua, near the southeast end of the island. Campsites located along small dunes bordering beach. Activities here include swimming. Also baseball and basketball facilities, picnic tables, and showers and restrooms.

Bellows Field Beach Park. Situated off Kalanianaole Hwy. (72), approximately 1½ miles north of Waimanalo Beach (southeast of Kailua). 46-acre park, quite popular with families for weekend camping. The park also has a long, white-sand beach, backed by ironwood trees, with the campsites located amid the trees. Swimming, surfing, and fishing. Picnic tables, showers, restrooms. Open from 12 p.m. Friday until 8 a.m. Monday.

Kualoa Regional Park. Located along Kamehameha Hwy. (83), 3½ miles north of Waiahole, on the Windward Coast. 150-acre park. Campsites situated on a broad lawn area dotted with palm trees, directly above a coral-lined beach. Views of Kaneohe Bay and Chinaman's Hat; some swimming possibilities. Park facilities include a lifeguard, and picnic tables, showers and restrooms. Open 7 a.m.-7 p.m.

Kaiaka State Recreation Area. Located on the North Shore, off Haleiwa Rd. (which goes off Kamehameha Hwy., 83), in Haleiwa. The campsites are situated in a large lawn area dotted with ironwood trees, directly above a small beach. Facilities include picnic tables, and restrooms.

Mokuleia Beach Park. Located on Farrington Hwy. (930), 4½ miles west of Waialua, just to the west of the North Shore. 12-acre beach park, with a long, narrow beach, backed by small sand dunes and a large, grassy area with campsites. Some windsurfing possibilities. Facilities include picnic tables, showers and restrooms.

HIKING

Honolulu Area Trails

Kanealole Trail. Tantalus area trail, with the trailhead located at the upper end of the Division of Forestry base yard; reached by way of Makiki Dr. north from Honolulu some 2½ miles, then Makiki Heights Dr. another 3/4 mile to the base yard. This is a moderate, 3/4-mile trail, which climbs approximately 500 feet to intersect with the Makiki Valley Trail, passing through lush vegetation, including ginger plants and guava and banana trees.

Maunalaha Trail. The trailhead for this trail is also located at the top end of the Division of Forestry base yard in the Tantalus area, adjacent to the Kanealole trailhead; reached on Makiki Dr. north from Honolulu to Makiki Heights Dr., some 2½ miles, then Makiki Heights Dr. another 3/4 mile to the base yard. 3/4-mile trail; journeys alongside the Kanealole Stream, through tropical wilderness —including groves of eucalyptus and bamboo—and, like the Kanealole Trail, also emerges on the Makiki Valley Trail. Views of Honolulu and the valley below.

Makiki Valley Trail. The trailhead is situated along the east side of Tantalus Rd. in Tantalus, 2 miles north of the intersection of Makiki Heights Dr. Easy, 1-mile trail, passing through Makiki Valley, east to west, crossing over a series of small streams and winding past groves of eucalyptus, kukui nut, guava and mountain apple trees, as well as ginger plants.

Makiki Valley Loop Trail. Moderate, 2-mile, Tantalus area trail, which essentially combines the Kanealole, Makiki Valley and Maunalaha trails.

Manoa Cliffs Trail. Moderate, 3-mile trail, which sets out from the north side of Tantalus Rd. in the Tantalus area, some 3 miles north of the intersection of Makiki Heights Dr., then journeys around Tantalus Mountain and its cliffs, to emerge on Round Top Dr., ½ mile from the trailhead—or the starting point. This is a particularly well maintained trail, frequently used by botany students from the University of Hawaii, lined with a variety of plants and trees—including hibiscus and mountain apple and koa trees—all tagged for easy identification.

Pu'u Ohia Trail. The Pu'u Ohia trailhead is also located on the north side of Tantalus Dr., ½ mile from the Manoa Cliffs trailhead. This is a moderate, 2-mile trail, which traverses Tantalus Mountain, passing by various ferns and trees, including eucalyptus, Norfolk Pine, guava and bamboo. Views from the summit, of Nu'uanu Valley and the Windward Coast.

Manoa Falls Trail. Located in the Manoa Valley; reached by following Manoa Rd. northeast from Honolulu, some 3 miles, to the very end. Easy, 3/4-mile trail, passing through tropical wilderness to lead to the 100-foot Manoa Falls, with its small, natural pool beneath, ideal for swimming. This is one of Oahu's most popular trails.

Aihualama Trail. Also situated in Manoa Valley, approximately 3 miles northeast of Honolulu, with the trailhead located along the Manoa Falls Trail, some 50 feet before reaching the falls. This is a somewhat strenuous trail, journeying 1½ miles to the Pu'u Ohia and Manoa Cliffs trails junction, passing by groves of bamboo and banyan trees, and through a koa forest.

Aiea Loop Trail. The trailhead is located in the Keaiwa Heiau State Recreation Area, reached by way of Aeia Heights Dr.—which goes off Moanalua Rd. (Hwy. 78) near the Moanalua Gardens of Honolulu—some 2½ miles northeast of Pearl Harbor. This is a popular, 4.8-mile trail that journeys around a hillside, passing through groves of Norfolk Pine, eucalyptus and ironwood trees. Also along the trail are the ancient Keaiwa Heiau and the remains of the wreckage of a C-47 cargo plane that crashed here in 1943. Park hours: 7 a.m.-7.45 p.m. daily.

East Honolulu

Diamond Head Crater Hike. Situated at the southeast end of Waikiki, with the entrance to the crater located off Diamond Head Rd. (which goes off Kalakaua Ave.), near 18th Ave., from where a ½-mile drive leads to the floor of the crater. From the crater floor, a 3/4-mile, moderately strenuous trail leads to Leahi—the peak of the crater rim, with an elevation of 760 feet—winding along a series of switchbacks and climbing some 200 steps through two dark tunnels —for which a flashlight is recommended. There is a lookout at Leahi, with sweeping views of the Pacific Ocean. Crater hours: 6 a.m.-6 p.m. daily.

Oahu

Waianae Coast

Kaena Point Trail. Situated in the Kaena Point Natural Area Reserve at the northwest corner of the island; reached directly on Farrington Hwy. (93), some 5½ miles northwest of Makaha. The trail begins at the end of the highway (93), and leads along a flat stretch of land to Kaena Point, the westernmost point on Oahu. Moderate, 2-mile trail. Ocean views from Kaena Point.

GOLF COURSES

Hawaii Country Club. Kunia Rd., Wahiawa; (808) 621-5654. 18 holes, par 72, 5,761 yards. Green fees: $75.00 weekends, $70.00 weekdays, $40.00 (including cart) after 4 p.m. Pro shop, club rentals, driving range; also restaurant.

Hawaii Kai Golf Course. 8902 Kalanianaole Hwy., Honolulu; (808) 395-2358. Offers two 18-hole courses: a 6,686-yard, par-72 championship course; and 2,433-yard, par-55 executive course. Green fees: $100.00 (including cart) for the championship course, $50.00 after 4 p.m.; and $37.50 for the executive course, $10.00 after 4 p.m. Facilities include a pro shop with club rentals, and a driving range and restaurant.

Hawaii Prince Golf Club. 91-1200 Fort Weaver Rd., Ewa Beach; (808) 689-8361. 27-hole, Arnold Palmer-designed championship course; par 72, 7,000 yards. Green fees: $135.00 (including cart rental) for 18 holes, and $20.00 for the additional 9 holes. Pro shop on premises; also driving range, and restaurant.

Kahuku Golf Course. Off Kamehameha Hwy., Kahuku; (808) 293-5842. 9-hole municipal course in oceanfront setting. Par 35, 2,699 yards. Green fees: $20.00 for 9 holes, $40.00 for 18 holes. No carts.

Ko Olina Golf Course. 92-1220 Aliinui Dr., Ewa Beach; (808) 676-5309. Ted Robinson-designed course; 18 holes, par 72, 6,900 yards. Green fees: $145.00 (including cart), $65.00 after 2.30 p.m. Pro shop, club rentals, driving range, and restaurant.

Makaha Valley Country Club. 84-627 Makaha Valley Rd., Makaha; (808) 695-7111. 18 holes, par 71, 6,091 yards. Green fees: $65.00/weekends, $55.00/weekdays (including cart). Driving range, pro shop, club rentals. Also restaurant.

Mililani Golf Club. 95-176 Kuahelani Ave., Mililani; (808) 623-2254. 18-hole course; par 72, 6,360 yards. Green fees: $89.00 before 11 a.m., $65.00 after 11 a.m; rates include cart rentals. Also pro shop on premises. Driving range, restaurant.

Olomana Golf Links. 41-1801 Kalanianaole Hwy., Waimanalo; (808) 259-7926. 18 holes, par 72, 5,856 yards. Green fees: $90.00 (including cart). Pro shop, club rentals, driving range, restaurant.

Pearl Country Club. 98-535 Kaonohi, Aiea; (808) 487-3802. 18 holes, par 72, 6,230 yards. Green fees: $80.00 weekends, $75.00 weekdays (for U.S. residents); $100.00 weekends, $95.00 weekdays (for foreign nationals). All rate include cart rentals. Also pro shop, club rentals, driving range. Restaurant.

Sheraton Makaha Resort West Golf Course. 84-626 Makaha Valley Rd., Makaha; (808) 695-9544. 18-hole championship course, rated one of the best on the island. 7,091 yards, par 72. Green fees: $160.00 (including cart). Pro shop, rentals, driving range, and restaurant.

Turtle Bay Hilton & Country Club. Kahuku; (808) 293-8574. 18-hole, oceanfront resort course; par 72, 6,366 yards. Green fees: $125.00, $75.00 twilight hours. Rates include cart rentals. Also pro shop, and club rentals. Driving range, snack bar.

West Loch Golf Course. 91-1126 Okupe St., Ewa Beach; (808) 671-2292 (296-5624). Municipal course with 18 holes; par 72, 6,070 yards. Green fees: $50.00, half price during twilight hours. Pro shop, club rentals, driving range; also snack bar.

TENNIS COURTS

Honolulu Tennis Club. 2220 S. King St., Honolulu; (808) 944-9696. Offers 4 tennis courts, including 2 with lights. Court fee: $8.00 per person.

Ilikai Sports Center. 1777 Ala Moana Blvd., Honolulu; (808) 949-3811, ext. 6428. 6 courts available for day use. Court fee: $7.50 per hour.

Sheraton Makaha Resort. 84-626 Makaha Valley Rd., Waianae; (808) 695-9511/(800) 325-3535. 4 courts with lights. Pro shop and restaurant on premises. Court fee: $12.00 per person per hour.

Turtle Bay Hilton & Country Club. Kamehameha Hwy., Kahuku; (808) 293-8811. 10 courts available, including 4 with lights; pro shop. Court fee: $10.00 per person per hour.

Public County Tennis Courts. *Ala Moana Tennis Courts.* 1201 Ala Moana Blvd., Honolulu; (808) 522-7031. 10 courts, with lights. *Diamond Head Tennis Center.* 3980 Paki Ave., Honolulu; (808) 971-7150. 10 courts, no lights. *Kapiolani Park.* 2755 Monsarrat Ave., Honolulu; (808) 971-2500. 4 courts with lights. *Koko Head District Park.* 423 Kaumakani, Honolulu; (808) 395-3096. 6 courts with lights.

TOURS

Helicopter Tours

Helicopter tours are quite popular on Oahu, and a good way to see the island, with tour companies offering flights over Pearl Harbor, and the island's Windward Coast and the North Shore. Tours generally originate at the Honolulu Airport in Honolulu. Typically, tour companies utilize any of three different types of helicopters—the Aero-Star, a 6-seater, with all six seats by the windows, offering good views to all passengers; the Hughes 500, a 4-seater, which also offers window seating to all passengers; and the Bell Jet Ranger, another 4-seater, which, nevertheless, has only three window seats, with one passenger being confined to a middle seat and, consequently, lesser views. Tours last anywhere from 20 minutes to an hour, and cost $80-$190 per person.

Helicopter Tour Companies. *Cherry Helicopters,* 410 Aowena Pl., Honolulu Airport, (808) 293-2570; *Hawaiian Odyssey Helicopters,* Honolulu Airport, (808) 833-4354; *Rainbow Pacific Helicopters,* Hololulu Airport, (808) 834-1111; *Makani Kai Helicopters,* Honolulu Airport, (808) 834-5813.

Oahu 101

Plane and Glider Tours

The Original Glider Rides. Dillingham Airfield, Mokuleia; (808) 677-3404. Offers 20-minute sightseeing flights, 10.30 a.m.-5 p.m. daily. Tour cost: $45.00 for one person, $70.00 for two persons. No reservations required.

Soar Hawaii. Dillingham Airfield, Mokuleia; (808) 637-3147. 20- and 30-minute glider flights; also acrobatic flights. Cost: glider rides for two persons, $70.00 for 20 minutes, $90.00 for 30 minutes; acrobatic flights per person, $100.00 for 20 minutes, $125.00 for 30 minutes.

Sightseeing Tours

E Noa Tours. 1110 University Ave., Room 306, Honolulu; (808) 599-2561/(800) 824-8804. Offers guided tours of Pearl Harbor, the Polynesian Cultural Center, Chinatown and downtown Honolulu, the Bishop Museum, and Waikiki. Also "circle island" tours, including in its itinerary the North Shore surfing beaches, Waimea Falls Park, and the Windward Coast. Cost of tours ranges from $14-$70.

Polynesian Adventure Tours. 1049 Kikowaena Pl., Honolulu; (808) 833-3000. Tours of the Arizona Memorial and the Polynesian Cultural Center; "Circle island" tours, including the North Shore and Waimea Falls Park, Diamond Head Crater, Hanauma Bay and the Windward Coast. Full-day and half-day tours. Also custom tours in mini coaches. Cost of tours: $15-$64 adults, $12-$35 children.

Roberts Hawaii Tours. 680 Iwilei Rd., Suite 700, Honolulu; (808) 539-9400. Variety of sightseeing tours and excursions, including Pearl Harbor, the Polynesian Cultural Center, the North Shore, Waimea Falls Park, Hanauma Bay, Windward Coast, the Pali Lookout, and even downtown Honolulu. Also "circle island" tours. Cost: $23-$42 adults, $11.50-$21.00 children.

Trans Hawaiian Oahu Tours. 720 Iwilei Rd., Suite 101, Honolulu; (808) 566-7300. Guided tours of Honolulu and Pearl Harbor, Paradise Park, Polynesian Cultural Center, Waimea Falls Park, and scenic Windward Coast. "Circle island" tours also offered. Tour cost: $25-$55 adults, $18-$35 children.

Bicycle Tours

Backroads of Hawaii. Honolulu; (808) 734-7827. Offers guided bike rides for beginners as well as advanced cyclists. Typically, beginner rides are 4-5 miles long, along the coast, with a moderate hike to a scenic lookout, and last approximately 1¼ hours; and advanced rides journey along the ridges of the North Shore, some 6 miles, and last roughly 2½ hours. Continental breakfast and a lunch on the beach are included in the itinerary. Free transportation from Honolulu and Waikiki.

Horseback Riding

Correa Trails Hawaii. 41-050 Kalanianaole Hwy.; (808) 259-9005. Guided trail rides along the Koolau Mountain Range.

Kualoa Ranch. 49-560 Kamehameha Hwy. (83), Ka'a'awa; (808) 237-7321. Guided horseback tours of the Ka'a'awa Valley, on Oahu's Windward Coast. Offered on weekends only. Cost: one-hour tour, $25.00; two-hour tour, $35.00.

102   Oahu

WATER SPORTS

(The *Hawaii Charter Skippers Association* offers a reservation service for sight seeing, whale watching, scuba diving, snorkeling and sport fishing trips. For additional information, call the *Association* at (808) 591-9100/(888) 908-9100.)

Boat Tours and Snorkeling Excursions

Atlantis Submarines. Departing from the Hilton Hawaiian Village, Waikiki; (808) 973-9811. Unique submarine excursions aboard a 65-foot submarine, exploring more than 100 feet below the ocean surface, along the reef just offshore from Waikiki Beach. 1-hour, 45-minute excursions. Tour cost: $89.00 per person.

Honolulu Sailing Co. 47-335 Lulani St., Kaneohe; (808) 239-3900. Offers half-day and full-day sailing excursions. Also overnight inter-island trips. Cost for half-day trip is $60.00 per person, and full-day trip $90.00 per person; overnight trips are $160.00 per person.

North Shore Catamaran Charters. Haleiwa Boat Harbor, Haleiwa; (808) 638-8279. 4-hour catamaran excursions, including snorkeling and a picnic lunch on a beach on Oahu's North Shore. 2-hour sunset cruises also available, and 2½-hour whale-watching excursions also offered, Jan.-Apr., with refreshments on board. Tour cost: 4-hour catamaran excursion, $54.00; whale-watching tour, $30.00; sunset cruise, $30.00.

Paradise Cruise. 350 Ward Ave., Suite 210, Honolulu; (808) 983-7700. 3-hour cruises of Waikiki and Pearl Harbor. Cost: $26.50 cruise only, $42.00 cruise with continental breakfast and buffet lunch. A 3-hour snorkeling cruise is also offered; it includes snorkeling and a barbeque lunch. Cost: $48.50.

Royal Hawaiian Cruises. Kewalo Basin, Honolulu; (808) 848-6360. Pearl Harbor, luncheon and sunset dinner cruises—with live entertainment—on board the 140-foot *Navatek I*. Tour cost for the 2-hour day cruise, $45.00 adults/ $26.00 children; sunset dinner cruises with 5-star meal $140.00 adults/$110 children.

Windjammer Cruises. Pier 7A, Aloha Tower, Honolulu; (808) 537-1122. Sunset and moonlight dinner cruises, with on-board dinner, cocktails, and a Polynesian show. Cost: $39.00 per person for Hawaiian buffet dinner, $69.00 for full service dinner, and $99.00 for steak and lobster dinner.

Scuba Diving

Scuba diving is a popular recreational sport in Oahu, with several different companies offering introductory scuba dives as well as tank dives for certified divers. Dives are offered both from the shore and from boats. Rates range from $100-$120 for introductory dives, to $90-$120 for tank dives; transportation and equipment are generally included.

Scuba Diving Outfitters and Operators. *Captain Bruce's Scuba Charters,* (808) 373-3590. *Ocean Works,* 2139 Kuhio Ave, #11, (808) 926-3483. *Bojac Aquatic Center,* (808) 671-0311. *South Seas Aquatic,* (808) 922-0852. *Aloha Dive Shop,* (808) 395-5922/395-8882.

Oahu

Surfing

Oahu is, of course, one of the most popular places in the United States for surfing, with scores of surf shops located there, offering an assortment of surfboards, boogie boards and wet suits for both rental and sale, as well as surf and beach reports. Following are some of the area surf shops, many of them located in close proximity to the beaches. *Local Motion,* 1714 Kapiolani Blvd., (808) 955-7873, Waikiki (808) 926-7873, Koko Marina (808) 396-7873, Waikele Center (808) 668-7873; *Blue Hawaii Surf,* cnr. McCully and Young Sts., Honolulu, (808) 955-2583; *Tropical Rush Surf Co.,* 62-620A Kamehameha Hwy., Haleiwa, (808) 627-8886; *Surf & Sea,* 62-595 Kamehameha Hwy., Haleiwa, (808) 637-9887.

Sportfishing

There are over a dozen or so companies offering sportfishing charters around Oahu, operating from different parts of the island. Charters, typically, last 4-8 hours, with prices ranging from $100-$150 per person for shared or group charters, to $600-$900 for exclusive trips; rates include all equipment, as well as beverages on the trips. For more information, and reservations, contact any of the following: *Alii Kai Sport Fishing,* Kewalo Basin, Honolulu; (808) 596-2443. *Blue Nun Sport Fishing,* Kewalo Basin, Honolulu; (808) 591-8889. *E.L.O.,* Kewalo Basin, Honolulu; (808) 947-5208. *Island Charters,* Kewalo Basin, Honolulu; (808) 593-8431. *Kamome Sport Fishing,* Kewalo Basin, Honolulu; (808) 593-8931. *Maggie Joe,* Kewalo Basin, Honolulu; (808) 591-8888. *Sea Verse,* Kewalo Basin, Honolulu; (808) 591-8840. *Pacific Blue Sport Fishing,* Kewalo Basin, Honolulu; (808) 396-4401. *Mary I,* Kewalo Basin, Honolulu; (808) 596-2998.

Kayaking

Bob Twogood Kayaks Hawaii. 171-B Hamakua Dr. Kailua; (808) 262-5656. Offers half-day and full-day kayak rentals on the Kailua coast. Kayaks are delivered to Kailua Beach, from where visitors can also explore the Moka Lua Islands, which are just offshore. Rental cost: single kayak $22.00/half day, $28.00/full day; double kayak $29.00/half day, $39.00/full day.

Parasailing

Parasailing is also quite popular on Oahu, with a few different companies offering flights. Typically, the cost for a 10-minute flight on an hour-long boat ride ranges from $39-$45. For more information, and reservations, contact any of the following: *Aloha Parasail,* Honolulu, (808) 521-2446; *Hawaii Kai Parasail,* Hawaii Kai Shopping Center, Honolulu, (808) 396-9224; or *Seabreeze Parasailing,* Honolulu, (808) 396-0100.

Windsurfing

Kailua Sailboard Company. 130 Kailua Rd., Kailua; (808) 262-2555. Sailboard rentals; also beginner lessons. Rentals: $25-$30 for half day, $30-$35 for full day, or $125-$150 per week. Lessons: $39.00 for 3-hour lesson.

104 Oahu

Naish Hawaii. 155-A Hamakua Dr., Kailua; (808) 262-6068. Offers windsurfing lessons, as well as sailboard rentals. Cost: rentals range from $30-$40 for full day to $150-$200 for a week; lessons range from $40-$55 per person.

Surf & Sea. 62-595 Kamehameha Hwy., Haleiwa; (808) 637-9887. Rentals of sailboards available. Also windsurfing lessons. Cost: hourly and full-day rentals, $15-$40; weekly rentals, $200.00; lessons, $40.00 for 2-hour lesson.

Waikiki Windsurfing. 2055 Kalaia Rd., Honolulu; (808) 949-8952. Sailboard rentals, and beginner lessons. Cost: rentals, $18-$50; lessons, $40.00 for 2-hour lesson.

Waterskiing

Suyderhoud Water Ski Center. Koko Marina Shopping Center, Honolulu; (808) 395-3773. 30- and 60-minute waterskiing tows. Also lessons for beginners. Cost: 30-minute tow, $59.00; 60-minute tow, $99.00; half-hour lesson, $65.00.

RESTAURANTS

(Restaurant prices—based on full course diner, excluding drinks, tax and tips—are categorized as follows: *Deluxe,* over $30; *Expensive,* $20-$30; *Moderate,* $10-$20; *Inexpensive,* under $10.)

Honolulu

Andrew's Restaurant. *Moderate-Expensive.* 1088 Bishop, Honolulu; (808) 539-3115. Contemporary island cuisine. Open for breakfast, lunch and dinner, and Sunday brunch. Reservations recommended.

Auntie Pasto's. *Moderate.* 1099 S. Beretania, Honolulu; (808) 523-8855. Authentic Italian cooking; pasta dishes, and chicken and vegetable specialties. Informal, European decor. Lunch and dinner daily. Reservations suggested.

Bon Appetit. *Moderate-Expensive.* Discovery Bay Shopping Center, 2170 Halekoa Dr., Honolulu; (808) 735-3821. French bistro setting. Specializes in French cuisine with a Hawaiian flavor, emphasizing fresh island ingredients. House specialties include veal stuffed with sweetbread, slow-roasted Ni'ihau whole rack of lamb, and broiled, wild Lanai red venison medallions. Also cocktails. Open for dinner. Reservations recommended.

California Pizza Kitchen. *Inexpensive-Moderate.* Kahala Mall Shopping Center, 4211 Waialae Ave., Honolulu; (808) 737-9446. Wide selection of pizzas, pasta and salads; also barbecued chicken and Peking duck. Casual atmosphere. Open for lunch and dinner.

Compadres Mexican Bar & Grill. Ward Centre, 1200 Ala Moana Blvd., Bldg. 3, Honolulu; (808) 591-8307. Traditional Mexican dishes, including fajitas, carnitas, and fresh fish. Contemporary, south-of-the-border decor; outdoor dining. Open for lunch and dinner daily.

Dew Drop Inn. *Inexpensive-Moderate.* 1088 S. Beretania, Honolulu; (808) 526-9522. Authentic Chinese cooking. Good selection of fish, beef and chicken entrees. House specialties include steamed tofu potstickers, Mongolian beef and lemon chicken. Casual atmosphere. Open for lunch and dinner.

Garden Cafe. *Inexpensive.* At the Honolulu Academy of Arts, 900 S. Beretania St., Honolulu; (808) 532-8734. Outdoor, courtyard setting. Serves primarily American fare, including sandwiches, salads and soups. Open for lunch daily.

Hoku's. *Expensive-Deluxe.* At the Kahala Mandarin Oriental, 5000 Kahala Ave., Honolulu; (808) 739-8777. Elegant, restaurant with ocean views. Serves Continental cuisine, including fresh island fish, and beef and chicken preparations with exotic sauces. Open for lunch and dinner. Reservations recommended.

Hard Rock Cafe. *Inexpensive-Moderate.* 1837 Kapiolani Blvd., Honolulu; (808) 955-7383. Informal cafe, decorated with Rock 'n Roll memorabilia. Standard American fare—burgers, steak, and fresh fish. Also cocktails. Open for lunch and dinner.

India Bazaar Madras Cafe. *Inexpensive.* 2320 S. King, Honolulu; (808) 949-4840. Authentic Indian cooking, featuring a variety of curries, and chicken, fish and vegetarian dishes. Informal setting. Lunch and dinner daily.

India House Restaurant. *Moderate-Expensive.* 2632 South King St., Honolulu; (808) 955-7552. Traditional Indian cuisine, featuring Kashmiri chicken, lamb virdaloo, fish masala, and a variety of curries and vegetarian dishes. Authentic Indian decor. Open for lunch and dinner daily. Reservations suggested.

John Dominis Restaurant. *Moderate-Expensive.* 43 Ahui St., Honolulu; (808) 523-0955. Spacious dining room, overlooking Waikiki Beach and Diamond Head. Offers fresh island fish, lobster, crab, and a variety of Japanese specialties; also homemade pasta. Entertainment, Open for dinner. Reservations suggested.

Keo's Thai Cuisine. *Moderate.* Offers two Honolulu locations: 625 Kapahulu Ave., (808) 737-8240; and Ward Centre, 1200 Ala Moana Blvd., (808) 596-0020. Popular Thai restaurants, serving traditional curries, and fresh island fish and vegetarian specialties. Open for dinner. Reservations suggested.

Like Like Drive-Inn. *Inexpensive.* 745 Keeaumoku St., Honolulu; (808) 941-2515. Established in 1953; informal setting. Offers a variety of "local" favorites, including saimin, sandwiches, salads, steak and lobster. Open 24 hours, daily.

Plumeria Beach Cafe. *Expensive.* At the Kahala Mandarin Oriental, 5000 Kahala Ave., Kahala; (808) 739-8776. Open-air setting. Serves extensive buffet lunch with salads and Japanese items. Dinner menu features fresh seafood, salads, pasta, chicken and veal. Excellent selection of desserts. Open for lunch and dinner daily. Reservations recommended.

Mekong I. *Inexpensive-Moderate.* 1295 South Beretania St., Honolulu; (808) 591-8841. Authentic Thai cuisine, served in intimate setting with Thai decor. House specialties include spicy curries with chicken, beef and seafood; also vegetarian curries. Open for dinner. Reservations suggested.

Mekong II. 1726 South King St., Honolulu; (808) 941-6184. Thai restaurant, serving spring rolls, satay, and a variety of spicy Thai curries; meat as well as vegetarian preparations. Open for dinner. Reservations suggested.

Ono Hawaiian Foods. *Inexpensive.* 726 Kapahulu Ave. Honolulu; (808) 737-2275. Established, informal restaurant, specializing in authentic Hawaiian cuisine. This is in fact one of the few places to sample Hawaiian food—including laulau, kalua pig and poi—besides luaus. Open for lunch and dinner daily.

Pagoda Restaurant. *Moderate-Expensive.* At the Pagoda Hotel, 1525 Rycroft St., Honolulu; (808) 941-6611. Garden setting. Serves primarily Continental and Oriental cuisine, including prime rib, Chinese-style roast duck, shrimp, and vegetable tempura. Also cocktails available. Open for breakfast, lunch and dinner.

Roy's Restaurant. *Moderate-Expensive.* At the Hawaii Kai Corporate Plaza, 6600 Kalanianaole Hwy., Honolulu; (808) 396-7697. Spacious dining room with ocean views. Specializing in Continental dishes, with a flavor of the Pacific Rim. House specialties include mesquite-smoked Peking duck, and Mongolian loin of lamb. Also pizzas, pasta, and fresh island seafood. Cocktails available. Open for dinner. Reservations recommended.

Salerno Ristorante Italiano. *Moderate.* McCully Shopping Center, 1960 Kapiolani, Suite 204, Honolulu; (808) 942-5273/946-3299. Traditional Italian dishes. House specialties include stuffed eggplant, chicken cacciatore, and homemade pasta. Lunch and dinner daily. Reservations suggested.

Sunset Grill. *Moderate.* Restaurant Row, 500 Ala Moana Blvd, #1A, Honolulu; (808) 521-4409. Contemporary California-style restaurant, featuring primarily American cuisine, including specialties from the wood-burning grill and open rotisserie. Menu emphasizes fresh pasta, fish and chicken; also baby back ribs. Open for lunch and dinner daily; brunch on weekends. Reservations recommended.

Wo Fat Restaurant. *Moderate.* 115 North Hotel St., Honolulu; (808) 524-1628. Honolulu's oldest restaurant, established in 1882. Features authentic Chinese cooking, with a good selection of fish, chicken, pork and beef dishes. Open for lunch and dinner. Reservations suggested.

Yen King. *Inexpensive-Moderate.* Kahala Mall Shopping Center, 4211 Waialae Ave., Honolulu; (808) 732-5505. Specializing in Northern Chinese cuisine. Features beef, pork, fowl and seafood dishes. Open for dinner. Reservations suggested.

Yum Yum Tree Kahala. *Inexpensive.* Kahala Mall Shopping Center, 4211 Waialae Ave., Honolulu; (808) 753-3544. Casual, family restaurant, serving primarily standard American fare—burgers, sandwiches, salads, chicken, fish. Also homemade pies. Open for breakfast, lunch and dinner.

Waikiki

Bali-by-the-Sea. *Expensive.* At the Hilton Hawaiian Village, Rainbow Tower, 2005 Kalia Rd., Honolulu; (808) 941-2254. Oceanfront restaurant, offering a blend of French and island cuisine. Good selection of seafood and steaks. Also cocktails, and entertainment. Open for dinner. Reservations suggested.

Banyan Veranda. *Moderate.* Sheraton Moana Surfrider Hotel, 2365 Kalakaua Ave, Honolulu; (808) 922-3111, ext.2382. Delightful, open-air setting, with views of Waikiki Beach and the ocean. Serves primarily American dishes. Entertainment. Open for breakfast, lunch, and afternoon tea; brunch on Sundays. Reservations suggested.

Beachcomber Restaurant. *Moderate-Expensive.* At the Waikiki Beachcomber Hotel, 2300 Kalakaua Ave., Honolulu; (808) 922-4646. Continental cuisine, with a flavor of the Orient. Specialties include shrimp scampi, mahimahi macadamia, breast of chicken with herbs, and New York steak. Also cocktails. Open for breakfast, lunch and dinner daily. Reservations suggested.

Benihana of Tokyo. *Expensive.* At the Hilton Hawaiian Village, Rainbow Bazaar, 2005 Kalia Rd. Honolulu; (808) 955-5955. Japanese cuisine, featuring Teppanyaki-style steak and seafood prepared at the tableside. Also Hibachi steak, and chicken preparations. Open for lunch and dinner. Reservations suggested.

California Pizza Kitchen. *Inexpensive-Moderate.* Canterbury Place, 1910 Ala Moana Blvd., #5, Honolulu; (808) 955-5161. Informal restaurant, specializing in pizza, salads and pasta. Open for lunch and dinner daily.

Cappuccinos. *Deluxe.* At the Waikiki Joy Hotel, 320 Lewers St., Honolulu; (808) 924-1530. Well-appointed gourmet restaurant. Menu features American, European, Southwestern and Pacific Rim cuisine, including char-broiled ahi, prime rib, and pasta dishes. Cocktails also available. Open for lunch and dinner. Reservations recommended.

Chez Michel. *Deluxe.* At the Eaton Square Shopping Plaza, 444 Hobron Ln., Honolulu; (808) 955-7866. Elegant French restaurant. House specialties include escargot, fresh fish, veal medallions and breast of duck. Extensive wine list; also cocktails. Open for lunch and dinner. Reservations recommended.

Oahu

Ciao! An Italian Restaurant. *Moderate.* At the Sheraton Waikiki Hotel, 2255 Kalakaua Ave., Honolulu; (808) 922-4422, ext. 73140. Traditional Italian cooking, in contemporary setting. Offers a variety of pizzas and pasta dishes; also fresh fish preparations. Open for dinner. Reservations suggested.

Ciao Mein. *Moderate.* At the Hyatt Regency Waikiki, Ewa Tower, 2424 Kalakaua Ave., Honolulu; (808) 923-CIAO. Intimate, open-air restaurant, serving Chinese and Italian cuisine, including Black Bean Shrimp, roast duck, and a variety of pasta dishes. Also cocktails. Open for dinner. Reservations recommended.

Colony Steak and Seafood. *Expensive.* At the Hyatt Regency Waikiki, Diamond Head Tower, 2424 Kalakaua Ave., Honolulu; (808) 923-1234. Well-appointed Polynesian restaurant. Menu features fresh island fish, and steaks grilled over a kiawe-wood fire; also lobster, lamb and prime rib. Open for dinner. Reservations suggested.

Eggs 'n Things. *Inexpensive.* 1911-B Kalakaua Ave., Honolulu; (808) 949-0820. Omelettes, pancakes, waffles and crepes. Casual atmosphere. Open 11 a.m.-2 p.m. daily.

Golden Dragon. *Moderate-Expensive.* At the Hilton Hawaiian Village, Rainbow Tower, 2005 Kalia Rd., Honolulu; (808) 946-5336. Authentic Cantonese cuisine, served in garden setting overlooking tropical lagoon. House specialties include cold ginger chicken, lobster with curry sauce, and duck. Cocktails; entertainment. Open for dinner. Reservations suggested.

Prince Court. *Expensive-Deluxe.* At the Hawaii Prince Hotel, 100 Holomoana St., Honolulu; (808) 956-1111. Hawaiian regional and Continental cuisine, with beef, chicken, seafood, lamb, pasta and salad dishes. Open for lunch and dinner. Reservations suggested.

Hanohano Room. *Deluxe.* At the Sheraton Waikiki Hotel, 2255 Kalakaua Ave., Honolulu; (808) 922-4422. Well-appointed restaurant, overlooking Diamond Head and Waikiki Beach. Specializes in Continental cuisine. Good selection of seafood; also filet mignon and prime rib. Cocktails. Open for breakfast and dinner. Reservations recommended.

Hau Tree Lanai. *Moderate.* New Otani Kaimana Beach Hotel, 2863 Kalakaua Ave., Honolulu; (808) 921-7066. Overlooking San Souci Beach; open-air setting. Continental cuisine, featuring fresh island fish, pasta, London broil, and salads. Entertainment. Open for breakfast, lunch and dinner. Reservations suggested.

Hee Hing Restaurant. *Moderate.* At the Diamond Head Center, 449 Kapahulu Ave., Honolulu; (808) 735-5544. Informal Chinese restaurant. Menu features Peking duck, Mongolian beef, Hong Kong-style dim sum, and a variety of Hawaiian seafood. Lunch and dinner daily. Reservations suggested.

Hy's Steak House. *Expensive.* At Waikiki Park Heights Hotel, 2440 Kuhio Ave., Honolulu; (808) 922-5555. Well-regarded Waikiki steak house, specializing in char-broiled steaks, rack of lamb, veal, and fresh island fish. Cocktails, and entertainment. Intimate setting. Open for dinner. Reservations recommended.

Ilikai Yacht Club Restaurant & Bar. *Expensive.* At the Ilikai Hotel, 1777 Ala Moana Blvd., Honolulu; (808) 949-3811. Overlooking the Ala Wai Yacht Harbor. Continental cuisine. Menu features Jumbo Pacific Shrimp, lobster, prime rib, and fresh island seafood. Cocktails; entertainment. Open for dinner. Reservations suggested.

Kacho. *Moderate.* Waikiki Parc Hotel, 2233 Helumoa Rd., Honolulu; (808) 924-3535. Contemporary Japanese setting. Offers authentic Kyoto-style dinners, and a sushi bar. Open for breakfast, lunch and dinner. Reservations suggested.

Hanohano Room. *Moderate.* At the Sheraton Waikiki Hotel, 2255 Kalakaua Ave., Honolulu; (808) 922-4422 ext. 73321. Continental and Hawaiian cuisine. Open for breakfast and dinner daily; also Sunday brunch. Reservations suggested.

La Mer. *Deluxe.* At the Halekulani Hotel, Main Bldg., 2199 Kalia Rd., Honolulu; (808) 923-2311. Well-regarded oceanview restaurant, specializing in French cuisine. Menu features kiawe-smoked salmon, poached onaga with a three-caviar sauce, and grilled spicy opakapaka. Extensive wine list. Also cocktail lounge. Open for dinner. Jackets required; reservations recommended.

Lotus Moon Restaurant. *Moderate.* At the Sheraton Princess Kaiulani Hotel, Tower Wing, 120 Kaiulani Ave., Honolulu; (808) 931-4679. Peking, Shanghai and Szechuan cuisine. House specialties include shark fin soup with crabmeat, and braised abalone. Cocktails. Lunch and dinner daily. Reservations recommended.

Matteo's. *Expensive.* Marine Surf Hotel, 364 Seaside Ave., Honolulu; (808) 922-5551. Traditional Italian cuisine, including Italian sausage and peppers, and a good selection of pasta dishes. Also filet mignon, veal, rack of lamb, and live Maine lobster. Cocktails. Open for dinner. Reservations recommended.

Eastern Garden Restaurant. *Moderate.* At the Waikiki Terrace Hotel, 2045 Kalakaua Ave., Honolulu; (808) 955-6000. Authentic Mandarin and Cantonese cuisine. Open for lunch and dinner daily. Open for breakfast, lunch and dinner. Reservations suggested.

Michel's at the Colony Surf. *Deluxe.* At the Colony Surf Hotel, 2895 Kalakaua Ave., Honolulu; (808) 923-6552. Elegant French restaurant in oceanfront setting. Good selection of seafood and lobster; also some prime rib. Entertainment, cocktail lounge. Open for breakfast, lunch and dinner. Reservations recommended.

Miyako Restaurant. *Moderate.* At The New Otani Kaimana Beach Hotel, 2863 Kalakaua Ave., Honolulu; (808) 923-4739. Oceanview Japanese restaurant, with traditional tatami rooms as well as Western-style seating. Menu features fresh lobster, tempura, sushi and teppan dishes. Cocktails. Open for dinner. Reservations suggested.

Momoyama Restaurant. *Moderate.* At the Sheraton Princess Kaiulani Hotel, Tower Wing, 120 Kaiulani Ave., Honolulu; (808) 922-5811. Traditional Japanese cuisine, with good selection of fish, chicken and beef. Also sushi bar. Open for breakfast, lunch and dinner. Reservations recommended.

Monarch Room. *Deluxe.* At the Royal Hawaiian Hotel, 2259 Kalakaua Ave., Honolulu; (808) 931-7430. Well-appointed dining room, featuring Hawaiian monarchy-era decor. Offers Continental cuisine, with emphasis on fresh island fish, steak and prime rib. Live Hawaiian entertainment; cocktail bar. Open for dinner. Reservations recommended.

Monterey Bay Canners Outrigger. *Moderate.* At the Outrigger Waikiki Hotel, 2335 Kalakaua Ave., Honolulu; (808) 923-0711. Informal restaurant, serving primarily kiawe-broiled seafood, including lobster, scampi and mahimahi, and prime rib. Live entertainment. Open for breakfast, lunch and dinner daily. Reservations.

Musashi Restaurant. *Expensive.* At the Hyatt Regency Waikiki, Diamond Head Tower, 2424 Kalakaua Ave., Honolulu; (808) 923-1234. Authentic Japanese cuisine, in Oriental setting. Menu features fresh fish, island vegetables, and prime rib teriyaki. Also sushi bar, and teppanyaki grills. Open for breakfast and dinner. Reservations recommended.

Neptune's Garden Restaurant. *Expensive.* At the Pacific Beach Hotel, 2490 Kalakaua Ave., Honolulu; (808) 922-1233. Continental restaurant, with elegant decor and views of the indoor 3-story oceanarium. Menu features fresh island seafood and steaks. Extensive wine list. Open for dinner. Reservations recommended.

Nick's Fishmarket. *Expensive.* At the Waikiki Gateway Hotel, 2070 Kalakaua Ave., Honolulu; (808) 955-6333. Well-regarded Waikiki restaurant. Menu features fresh island seafood, steak, chicken and veal. Entertainment. Open for dinner. Reservations recommended.

Ocean Terrace. *Moderate.* At the Sheraton Waikiki Hotel, 2255 Kalakaua Ave., Honolulu; (808) 922-4422, ext. 72067. Open air, poolside setting, with ocean views. Features Continental buffets, and fresh island fish, steak, lobster, prime rib and salad bar. Cocktails. Open for breakfast, lunch and dinner. Reservations suggested.

Oceanarium Restaurant. *Inexpensive-Moderate.* At the Pacific Beach Hotel, 2490 Kalakaua Ave., Honolulu; (808) 922-1233. Casual, family-style restaurant, with a view of an indoor 3-story oceanarium. Offers Continental cuisine primarily, including seafood, steak and chicken. Also cocktails. Open for breakfast, lunch and dinner. Reservations suggested.

Orchids. *Moderate.* At Halekulani Hotel, 2199 Kalia Rd., Honolulu; (808) 923-2311. Oceanfront setting. American cuisine. House specialties include fresh island fish, roast duck and rack of lamb. Also offers dinner buffets, and cocktails. Open for breakfast, lunch and dinner, and brunch on Sundays. Reservations recommended.

Parc Cafe. *Moderate.* At the Waikiki Parc Hotel, 2233 Helumoa Rd., Honolulu; (808) 921-7272. Continental cuisine, served in a contemporary setting. Menu features fresh island seafood, roasted duck, chicken and lamb. Also cocktails. Breakfast, lunch and dinner daily. Reservations suggested.

Pikake Terrace Restaurant & Lounge. *Moderate-Expensive.* At the Sheraton Princess Kaiulani Hotel, 120 Kaiulani Ave., Honolulu; (808) 922-5811. Delightful poolside setting. Continental cuisine, with a wide selection of fresh fish, chicken and steak entrees. Entertainment. Open for breakfast, lunch and dinner. Reservations suggested.

Prince Court. *Expensive.* At the Hawaii Prince Hotel, 100 Holomoana St., Honolulu; (808) 956-1111. Well-appointed oceanview restaurant. Specializes in contemporary American cuisine, with an emphasis on Hawaiian and Pacific Rim ingredients. House specialties include seared and smoked ahi, taro leaf minestrone, and roasted rack of lamb in spicy crust. Cocktails. Breakfast, lunch and dinner daily. Reservations recommended.

Regent Hatsuhana. *Moderate.* At the Hawaiian Regent Hotel, 2552 Kalakaua Ave., Honolulu; (808) 922-6611. Japanese cuisine. Menu features fresh lobster, and tempura, sushi and teppan dishes. Private tatami rooms available. Open for breakfast, lunch and dinner. Reservations suggested.

Rigger Restaurant. *Inexpensive.* At the Outrigger Waikiki Hotel, 2335 Kalakaua Ave., Honolulu; (808) 922-5544. Casual family restaurant. Good selection of fresh island seafood and chicken; also steak, and fish and chips. Cocktails; entertainment. Breakfast, lunch and dinner daily.

The Secret. *Expensive.* Hawaiian Regent Hotel, 2552 Kalakaua Ave., Honolulu; (808) 921-5161. Well-appointed Waikiki restaurant, specializing in Continental and gourmet dishes, including roast duck with guava sauce, Scampi Provencale, and rack of lamb. Live entertainment; cocktails. Open for dinner. Reservations recommended; jackets required.

Sergio's Restaurant. *Expensive.* At the Ilima Hotel, 445 Nohonani St., Honolulu; (808) 926-3388. Elegant setting. Northern Italian cuisine. Specialties include homemade tortellini, fresh seafood, broiled veal chops and filet of venison. Open for dinner. Reservations suggested.

Ship's Tavern. *Expensive-Deluxe.* At the Sheraton Moana Surfrider, 2365 Kalakaua Ave., Honolulu; (808) 923-3111, ext. 2216. Elegant, oceanfront restaurant, serving contemporary Continental cuisine. House specialties include live Maine lobster, fresh island fish, filet mignon, and lamb. Open for dinner. Reservations recommended.

Shogun Restaurant. *Moderate.* At the Pacific Beach Hotel, 2490 Kalakaua Ave., Honolulu; (808) 922-1233. Authentic Japanese cuisine, with a good selection of fresh island seafood, lobster, and teriyaki dishes. Traditional Japanese decor. Open for breakfast, lunch and dinner. Reservations recommended.

Oahu

Surf Room. *Expensive.* At the Sheraton Royal Hawaiian Hotel, 2259 Kalakaua Ave., Honolulu; (808) 923-7311. Open-air restaurant, overlooking Waikiki Beach. Specializes in seafood buffets, and Continental cuisine. Hawaiian entertainment. Breakfast, lunch and dinner daily; also Sunday brunch. Reservations recommended.

Tahitian Lanai. *Moderate.* Aston Waikikian Hotel, 1811 Ala Moana Blvd., Honolulu; (808) 946-6541. Outdoor setting, with a lagoon and bamboo huts; Polynesian decor. Features American and Polynesian cuisine, with emphasis on fresh island seafood; also Maine lobster and Dungeness crab, and chicken curry. Cocktails; entertainment. Open for breakfast, lunch and dinner daily. Reservations suggested.

Takanawa Sushi Bar & Restaurant. *Expensive.* At the Hawaii Prince Hotel, 100 Holomoana St., Honolulu; (808) 956-1111. Casual, Japanese-style restaurant, in garden setting. Features Mizutaki and Yosenabe specialties, prepared at the table; also sushi bar. Open for dinner. Reservations recommended.

Tony Roma's A Place For Ribs. *Inexpensive-Moderate.* 1972 Kalakaua Ave., Honolulu; (808) 942-2121. American cuisine, featuring barbecued baby back ribs, Cajun-style chicken, and char-broiled island fish. Also cocktails. Open for lunch and dinner. Reservations suggested.

Trattoria. *Moderate.* At Edgewater Hotel, 2168 Kalia Rd., Honolulu; (808) 923-8415. Traditional Northern Italian dishes. Good selection of seafood, and pasta, chicken, veal and vegetarian entrees. Italian-Mediterranean decor, with Old World frescoes painted on the walls and ceilings. Open for dinner. Reservations suggested.

The Village Steak & Seafood Restaurant. *Moderate.* At the Hilton Hawaiian Village, Tapa Tower, 2005 Kalia Rd., Honolulu; (808) 949-4321, ext. 32. Informal setting. Serves primarily Continental cuisine. House specialties include steak, lobster, ginger-honey duck and Hawaiian chicken. Open for dinner. Reservation recommended.

W.C. Peacock & Company, Ltd. *Moderate.* At the Sheraton Moana Surfrider, Diamond Wing; 2365 Kalakaua Ave., Honolulu; (808) 922-3111, ext. 2218. Delightful setting, with ocean views. Menu features fresh island fish, filet mignon, Pacific lobster tails and chicken. Open for dinner. Reservations suggested.

Waikiki Broiler. *Moderate.* At the Outrigger Waikiki Towers. 200 Lewers St., Honolulu; (808) 923-8836. Open-air restaurant, in Hawaiian setting. Offers primarily standard American fare, including sandwiches, hamburgers, chicken, pasta, and a variety of seafood. Open for breakfast, lunch and dinner daily.

Central Oahu

Country Inn (Helemano Plantation). *Inexpensive.* 64-1510 Kamehameha Hwy., Wahiawa; (808) 622-3929. Situated adjacent to the Dole Plantation. Features a Chinese buffet, and a sandwich and fruit bar. Open for breakfast, lunch and dinner daily.

Dot's in Wahiawa. *Inexpensive.* 130 Mango St., Wahiawa; (808) 622-4115. Casual, local eatery, serving Japanese and American fare, including sandwiches and plate lunches. Also cocktails. Open for breakfast, lunch and dinner daily.

Elephant and Castle Restaurant. *Inexpensive.* In Newton Square, 98-1247 Kaahumanu St., Aiea; (808) 487-5591. Continental and English food, including fish and chips, seafood platters, and steak. Features classic, 16th-century English decor. Open for breakfast on weekends, and lunch and dinner daily.

Oahu

North Shore

The Cove. *Expensive.* At the Turtle Bay Hilton Hotel & Country Club, 55071 Kamehameha Hwy., Kahuku; (808) 293-8811, ext. 36. Intimate setting; spectacular sunsets. Features contemporary island cuisine, with emphasis on fresh seafood and homemade pasta dishes; also live Maine lobster. Cocktails; entertainment. Open for dinner Tues-Sat. Reservations recommended.

Cafe Haleiwa. *Inexpensive.* 66-460 Kamehameha Hwy., Haleiwa; (808) 637-5516. Popular local eatery, decorated with surfing photographs and memorabilia. Offers primarily pancakes, omelettes, burgers and sandwiches. Open for breakfast and lunch.

Jameson's by the Sea. *Moderate.* 62-540 Kamehameha Hwy., Haleiwa; (808) 637-4336. Open-air restaurant with tropical decor, overlooking Haleiwa Bay. Menu features fresh island seafood, including ono, mahimahi and opakapaka, as well as Australian lobster and filet mignon. Open for lunch and dinner. Reservations suggested.

Kua Aina Sandwich. *Inexpensive-Moderate.* 66-214 Kamehameha Hwy., Haleiwa; (808) 637-6067. Hamburgers, sandwiches and salads. Informal atmosphere, with walls covered with North Shore and surfing photographs. Open for lunch and dinner daily.

Rosie's Cantina. *Inexpensive-Moderate.* Haleiwa Shopping Plaza, Haleiwa; (808) 637-3538. Authentic Mexican and American food, including Spanish omelettes, breakfast burritos, burgers, sandwiches, grilled mahimahi, and seafood enchiladas. Open for breakfast, lunch and dinner.

Windward Coast

The Crouching Lion Inn. *Moderate-Expensive.* 51-666 Kamehameha Hwy., Ka'a'awa; (808) 237-8511. Open-air restaurant with ocean views, featuring English and Hawaiian decor. House specialties include Polynesian Shrimp, scallops and lobster tail, steak, filet mignon, and Coconut Island chicken. Live entertainment. Lunch and dinner daily. Reservations recommended.

Jaron's. *Moderate.* 201-A Hamakua Dr., Kailua; (808) 261-4600. Continental cuisine, in contemporary setting. Good selection of fresh fish, steak, chicken and pasta dishes. House specialties include scallops, bouillabaisse, and pepper steak Madagascar. Open for lunch and dinner. Reservations.

L'Auberge Swiss. *Moderate.* 117 Hekili St., Kailua; (808) 263-4663. Country inn atmosphere. Serves primarily Continental dishes, including filet mignon, veal scallopine, fresh fish and wienerschnitzel. Open for dinner. Reservations suggested.

Orson's Bourbon House. *Moderate.* 5 Hoolai St., Kailua; (808) 262-2306. Well-regarded restaurant, specializing in Cajun, Creole and international cuisine. Favorites here are blackened shrimp, fresh Cajun chicken, filet mignon, prime rib, and rack of lamb. Entertainment. New Orleans decor. Open for lunch and dinner. Reservations recommended.

Waianae Coast

Ka'ala Dining Room. *Moderate.* At the Sheraton Makaha Resort & Country Club, Main Bldg., 84-626 Makaha Valley Rd., Makaha; (808) 695-9511, ext. 7654. Specializing in Continental dishes, broiled steak, and fresh island seafood. Cocktails. Open for breakfast, lunch and dinner. Reservations suggested.

LUAUS

Ali'i Luau. Polynesian Cultural Center, Kamehameha Hwy., Laie; (808) 293-3333/923-1861/(800) 367-7060. Authentic Hawaiian and Polynesian foods, and spectacular Polynesian show, featuring more than a hundred performers. Luaus begin at 5.45 p.m., Mon.-Sat. Cost: $54.00 per person. Reservations suggested.

Paradise Cove Luau. At the Ko Olina Resort, 91-100 Kamoana Pl., Ewa Beach; (808) 775-2683/973-5828. Lavish Hawaiian buffets, with traditional Polynesian foods. Hawaiian music and dance. Luaus begin at 5.30 p.m., daily. Cost: $44.50 per person. Free shuttle from Waikiki. Reservations recommended.

Royal Hawaiian Luau. At the Royal Hawaiian Hotel, 2259 Kalakaua Ave., Honolulu; (808) 931-7194. Traditional Hawaiian luau, with an imu ceremony. Also Hawaiian music, and entertainment. Begins at 6 p.m., Mondays only. Cost: $63.00 per person. Reservations recommended.

HAWAIIAN GLOSSARY

The Hawaiian language, in its simplicity, contains only seven consonants — H, K, L, M, N, P, W — and five vowels — A, E, I, O and U. All words — and syllables — end in a vowel, and all syllables begin with a consonant. The vowels, typically, are each pronounced separately — i.e., *a'a* is pronounced "ah-ah," and *e'e* is pronounced "ay-ay"; the only exceptions are the diphthong double vowels — *ai,* pronounced "eye," and *au,* pronounced "ow." The consonants, on the other hand, are never doubled.

Hawaiian consonants are pronounced similar to those in English, with the notable exception of W, which is sometimes pronounced as "V," when it begins the last syllable of the word. Hawaiian vowels are pronounced as follows: A - "uh," as in among; E - "ay," as in day; I - "ee," as in deep; O - "oh," as in no; U - "oo," as in blue.

For travellers to the Hawaiian islands, the following is a glossary of some commonly used words in the Hawaiian language.

a'a — rough, crumbling lava.
ae — yes.
ahi — tuna fish.
ahupua'a — pie-shaped land division, extending from the mountains to the sea.
aikane — friend.
alanui — road, or path.
ali'i — a Hawaiian chief or nobleman.
aloha — love, or affection; traditional Hawaiian greeting, meaning both welcome and farewell.
anu — cold, cool.
a'ole — no.
auwe — alas!
awawa — valley.

hala — the pandanus tree, the leaves of which are used to make baskets and mats.
hale — house.
hale pule — church; house of worship.
hana — work.
hahana — hot, warm.
haole — foreigner; frequently used to refer to a Caucasian.
hapa — half, as in *hapa-haole*, or half Caucasian.
haupia — coconut cream pudding, often served at a luau.
heiau — an ancient Hawaiian place of worship; shrine, temple.
holoholo — to go for a walk; also to ride or sail.
honi — a kiss; also, to kiss.
hui — a group, society, or assembly of people.
hukilau — a communal fishing party, in which everyone helps pull in the fishing nets.
hula — traditional Hawaiian dance of storytelling.

Glossary

imu — underground oven, used for roasting pigs for luaus.
ipo — sweetheart, or lover.

ka'ahele — a tour.
ka'ao — legend.
kahuna — priest, minister, sorcerer, prophet.
kai — the sea.
kakahiaka — morning.
kama'aina — native-born, or local.
kanaka — man, usually of Hawaiian descent.
kane — male, husband.
kapu — taboo, forbidden; derived from the Tongan word, tabu.
keiki — child; a male child is known as *keikikane*, and a female child, *keikiwahine*.
kiawe — Algaroba tree, with fern-like leaves and sharp, long thorns, usually found in dry areas near the coast. Kiawe wood is used to make charcoal for fuel. The tree was introduced to Hawaii in the 1820s.
koa — native Hawaiian tree, prized for its wood which was used by early Hawaiians to craft canoes, spears and surfboards. Koa wood is now used to make fine furniture.
kokua — help.
kona — leeward side of island; frequently used to describe storms and winds, such as kona storm or kona wind. Also, south.
ko'olau — windward side of island.
kukui — Candlenut tree, characteristic in its yellow and green foliage, generally found in the valleys. Kukui nuts are also used in leis. Kukui is Hawaii's state tree.
kuleana — home site, or homestead; also responsibility, or one's business.
kupuna — grandparent.

lamalama — torch fishing
lanai — porch, veranda, balcony.
lani — the sky, or heaven
laulau — wrapped package; generally used to describe bundles of pork, fish or beef, served with taro shoots, wrapped in ti or banana leaves, and steamed.
lei — garland, wreath, or necklace of flowers.
lilikoi — passion fruit.
limu — seaweed.
luau — traditional Hawaiian feast.

mahalo — thanks, or thank you.
mahimahi — dolphin.
maile — native vine with shiny, fragrant leaves used in leis.
makahiki hou — New Year; *hauoli makahiki hou*, Happy New Year.

Glossary

make — to die, or dead.
makai — toward the ocean, or seaward.
malihini — stranger, newcomer.
mana — supernatural power.
manu — bird.
mauka — toward the mountain, or inland.
mauna — mountain.
mele — song, chant.
menehune — Hawaii's legendary little people, ingenious and hardworking, who worked only at night, building fishponds, heiaus, irrigation ditches and roads, many of which remain today.
moana — the ocean; open sea.
mo'o — lizard, dragon, serpent.
mu'umu'u — long, loose, traditional Hawaiian dress.

nani — beautiful.
nui — big.

ohana — family.
ono — delicious.

pakalolo — marijuana.
palapala — book; also printing.
pali — cliff; also plural, cliffs.
paniolo — Hawaiian cowboy.
pau — finished, all done.
poi — a purplish paste made from pounded and cooked taro roots; staple of Hawaiian diet.
puka — hole, opening.
pupu — appetizer, snack, hors d'oeuvre.
pupule — crazy; insane.

tapa — cloth made from beaten bark, often used in Hawaiian clothing.
taro — broad-leafed plant with starch root, used to make poi; staff of life of early Hawaiians, introduced to the islands by the first Polynesians.
ti — broad-leafed plant, brought to Hawaii by early Polynesian immigrants. *Ti* leaves are used for wrapping food as well as offerings to the gods.

waha — mouth; *waha nui*, a big mouth.
wahine — female, woman, wife.
wai — fresh water.
wiki — to hurry; *wikiwiki*, hurry up.

HAWAIIAN FLOWERS

HAWAIIAN FLOWERS

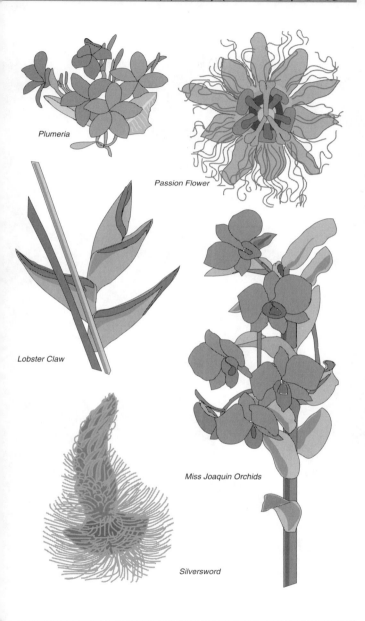

HAWAIIAN SEASHELLS

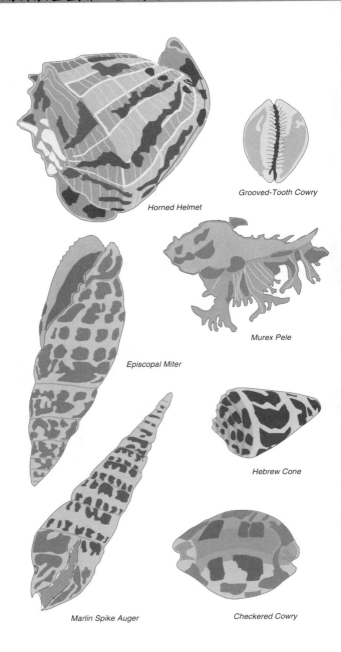

HAWAIIAN SEASHELLS

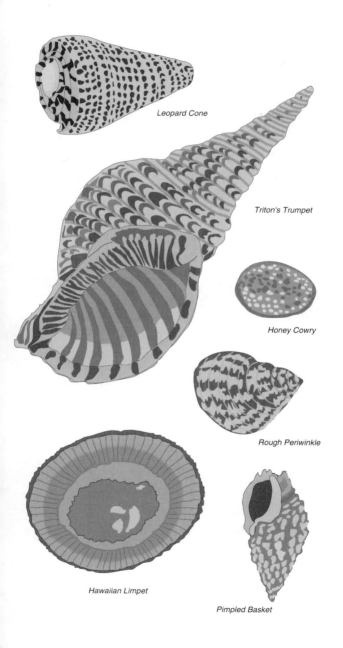

HAWAIIAN REEF FISH

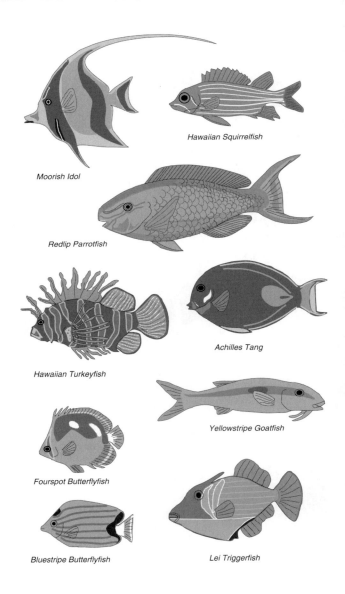

HAWAIIAN REEF FISH

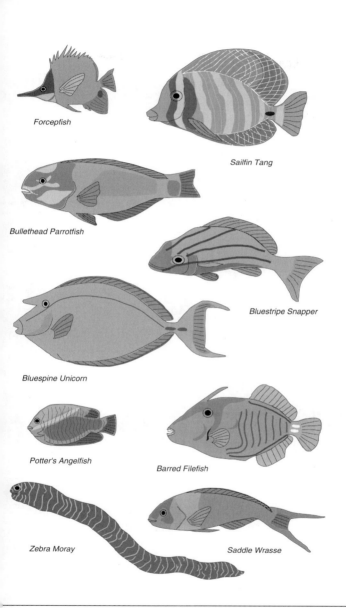

HAWAIIAN GAME FISH

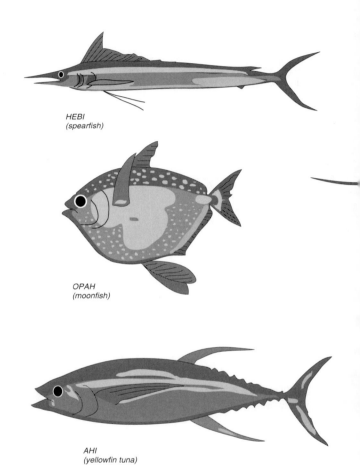

HEBI
(spearfish)

OPAH
(moonfish)

AHI
(yellowfin tuna)

HAWAIIAN GAME FISH

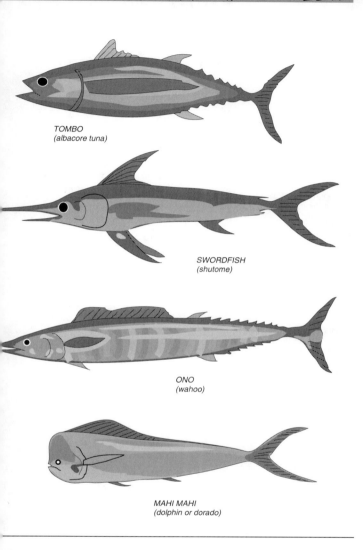

TOMBO
(albacore tuna)

SWORDFISH
(shutome)

ONO
(wahoo)

MAHI MAHI
(dolphin or dorado)

INDEX

Academy of Arts, 26
Accommodations, 69–74
Aiea Loop Trail, 98
Aihualama Trail, 34, 98
Aina Haina, 43
Aina Moana Beach Park,
    28, 82, 89
Ala Moana Beach Park, 28,
    89
Ala Moana Shopping Center,
    28, 82
Ala Wai Canal, 16, 28, 36
Alexander & Baldwin
    Building, 26
Aliiolani Hale, 22, 80
Aloha Tower, 28, 82
Automobile Rentals, 68

Banzai Pipeline,
    18, 50, 54, 87
Barbers Point Beach Park,
    62, 94–95
Battery Randolph, 38
Battleship Row, 16
Beaches, 89–96
Bed & Breakfast Inns, 74
Bellows Air Force Station,
    16
Bellows Field Beach Park,
    61, 94, 97
Bicycle Tours, 101
Bingham, Hiram, 14, 22
Bishop, Bernice Pauahi, 32
Bishop, Charles Reed, 32
Bishop Museum, 19, 32, 81
Boat Tours, 102
Brown, William, 14
Byodo-In Temple, 60, 88

Campgrounds, 96–97
Central Oahu, 47–55
Chamberlain House, 23
Chinatown, 19, 26-28, 80–81
Chun's Reef, 52, 92
City Hall, see Honolulu Hale
Contemporary Museum,
    33, 82
Cook, Captain James, 14
Cooke, Mrs. Montagne,
    26, 33
Crouching Lion, 58
Crouching Lion Inn, 58

Del Monte Pineapple Variety
    Garden, 49, 86
Diamond Head, 13, 19, 42
Diamond Head Crater, 42,
    84

Diamond Head Crater Hike,
    98
Dillingham Airfield, 52
Dillingham Building, 26
Dixon, George, 14
Dole Cannery Square, 82
Dole, James D., 16
Dole Plantation, 49, 86
Dole, Sanford B., 15
Dominis, John, 23
Downtown Honolulu,   19-
    25, map 24-25
Duke Kahanamoku, 36
Duke Kahanamoku Beach,
    36, 90

Earhardt, Amelia, 42
East Honolulu, 43–45, map
    44
Ehukai Beach Park, 54, 92
Ewa, 62
Ewa Beach, 62
Ewa Beach Park, 94

Falls of Clyde, 28, 82
Father Damien, 23
Fort DeRussy, 16, 36-
    38, 83
Fort DeRussy Beach Park,
    38, 90
Foster Botanic Garden, 29,
    32, 81
Foster, Captain Thomas, 32

Garden of the Missing, 29
Goat Island, 55
Golf Courses, 99–100
Gray's Beach, 38, 90

Haleiwa, 50
Haleiwa Ali'i Beach Park,
    50, 91
Haleiwa Beach Park, 52, 92
Halekulani Hotel, 16, 36, 38
Hall of Discovery, 32
Halona Blowhole, 45
Halona Cove, 45, 84, 91
Hanauma Bay, 43
Hanauma Bay Beach Park,
    84, 91
Hau'ula, 57
Hau'ula Beach Park, 57, 93
Hawaii Kai, 43
Hawaii Maritime Center, 28,
    82
Hawaii Mormon Temple, 55–
    57, 87
Hawaii Prince, 36

Index
125

Hawaii State Library, 23, 80
Hawaiian Electric Company
Building, 26
Hawaiian Publishing
Building, 26
Hawaiian Regent, 17
He'eia Fishpond, 59
He'eia State Park, 59, 88
Helicopter Tours, 100
Hemmeter, Chris, 40
Hi'iaka, 59
Hiking, 97–99
Hilton Hawaiian Village,
17, 36
History of Oahu, 13–19
Hockney, David, 33
Hokulea, 28
Honolulu, 19–35, *map* 30-
31
Honolulu Academy of Arts,
81
Honolulu Hale, 23, 80
Honolulu Harbor, 28
Honolulu Waterfront, 28–29
Honolulu Zoo, 41, 83
Ho'omaluhia Botanical
Garden, 60, 88
Horseback Riding, 101
Hotels, *see*
Accommodations
How to Get Around, 68
How to Get There, 67
Huila Pond, 58
Hyatt Regency Waikiki, 17,
40

Ilikai Hotel, 36
Inspiration Point, 34
Inter-island Flights, 67
International Marketplace,
39, 83
Iolani Barracks, 22, 79
Iolani Palace,
15, 19, 22, 79
Ironwood Avenue, 49–50
Izumo Taisha Shrine, 27

Judd, Gerrit, 14, 23
Judd Trail, 35

Ka'a'awa, 58
Ka'a'awa Beach Park, 93
Kaena Point, 52
Kaena Point Natural Area
Preserve, 66, 89, 96
Kaena Point Trail, 99
Kahala, 43
Kahalu'u Fishpond, 59
Kahana Bay, 58
Kahana Bay Beach Park,
58, 93, 96
Kahana Valley State Park, 58

Kahe Point Beach Park,
62, 95
Kahuku, 55
Kahuku Point, 55
Kahuku Sugar Mill, 87
Kahuku Sugar Mill Shopping
Center, 55
Kaiaka State Recreation
Area, 50, 91–92, 97
Kailua, 35, 55, 60
Kailua Beach Park, 60, 94
Kaiona Beach Park, 61, 94
Kaiwi Channel, 45
Kalaeolio Beach Park, 58, 93
Kalakaua, David, 15
Kalanianaole, Prince Jonah
Kuhio, 15
Kaliuwa'a Falls, *see* Sacred
Falls
Kamehameha I,
14, 22, 29, 35, 64, 65
Kamehameha IV, 23, 34
Kamehameha V, 15, 22
Kane, 14
Kaneaki Heiau, 65, 89
Kanealole Trail, 33, 97
Kaneana Cave, 66
Kane'ilio Point, 64
Kaneloa, 14
Kanenelu Beach, 59, 93
Kaneohe, 35, 55, 60
Kaneohe Marine Corps Air
Station, 16
Kaohikaipu Island, 46
Kapiolani, 22
Kapiolani Beach Park, 40-
41, 83, 90
Kauhi'imakaokalani, *see*
Crouching Lion
Kaupo Beach Park, 61, 94
Kawaiahao Church,
14, 22, 80
Kawailoa Beach, 52
Kayaking, 103
Kea'au Beach Park, 65–66,
96
Keaiwa Heiau, 47
Keaiwa Heiau State
Recreation Area,
47, 86, 96
Kealohi Point, 59
King Kalakaua, 19, 22
King Kamehameha II, 22
Kodak Hula Show, 41, 84
Koko Crater, 45
Koko Crater Botanical
Gardens, 45
Koko Crater, 84
Koko Head, 13, 43
Konahuanui, 13
Ko'olau Mountain Range, 13,
18, 19, 35, 47, 55

Index

126

Korean War, 29
Ku, 14
Kualoa Regional Park,
 59, 88, 93, 97
Kualoa Sugar Mill, 59
Kuan Yin Temple, 27
Kuhio Beach Park, 40, 90
Kuilei Cliffs Beach Park,
 42, 90
Kuilima Cove, 54, 92
Kuilioloa, 64
Kuilioloa Heiau, 64, 89
Kukaniloko Birth Stones, 49

Laie, 57
Laie Point, 57
Lanakila Church, 57
Laniakea Beach, 52, 92
Lanikai Beach, 60, 94
Leilehua Plateau,
 13, 15, 16
Liliuokalani Church, 52, 87
Lono, 14
Loomis, Elisha, 14, 23
Lua, 13
Lualualei Beach Park, 64,
 95
Luaus, 112
Lunalilo Mausoleum, 22
Lunalilo, William, 15, 29
Lyon Arboretum, 34, 82–83
Lyon, Harold L., 34

Magic Island, see Aina
 Moana Beach Park
Maili Beach Park, 64, 95
Makaha, 64
Makaha Beach Park, 65, 96
Makaha Valley, 65
Makapu'u Beach Park,
 45, 91, 97
Makapu'u Lighthouse, 45
Makapu'u Point, 45, 55, 61
Makiki Valley Loop Trail., 98
Makiki Valley Trail, 33, 98
Makua Beach, 66, 96
Malaekahana Bay State
 Recreation Area,
 55, 93, 96
Mamala Bay, 19
Manana Island, 46
Manners Beach, 62, 95
Manoa Cliffs Trail, 33, 98
Manoa Falls Trail, 34, 98
Manoa Valley, 19, 33, 34
Marquesans, 13–14
Mauna Lahilahi, 65
Mauna Lahilahi Beach Park,
 95
Maunalaha Trail, 33, 97
Maunalua Bay Beach Park,
 43, 91

Menehune, 53, 58, 59, 61
Merrie Monarch, see
 Kalakaua, David
Mission Houses Museum,
 23, 80
Moana Hotel, 16, 36
Moanalua Gardens, 47, 85
Mokoli'i Island, also
 Chinaman's Hat, 59, 88
Moku Auia, 55
Moku o Loe, also Coconut
 Island, 59
Mokuleia Beach Park,
 52, 91, 97
Moli'i Fishpond, 59
Motels, see
 Accommodations
Mount Ka'ala, 13, 18, 62

Nanakuli, 62
Nanakuli Beach Park,
 62, 95
Natatorium War Memorial,
 41, 84
National Memorial Cemetary
 of the Pacific, 29, 81–82
Niu Valley, 43
North Shore, 50–55, map 51
Nu'uanu Pali Lookout,
 35, 83
Nu'uanu Valley, 33, 35

Oahu, 18-113, map 20-21,
 practical information 67-
 113
Oahu Market, 27
Old Federal Building, 26
Organic Act, 15
Our Lady of Peace
 Cathedral, 26, 80

Pacific Whaling Museum, 45
Palace Grounds, 19
Pali Highway, 34
Papa, 13
Papaoneone Beach,
 65, 95–96
Parasailing, 103
Pearl City, 47–48
Pearl Harbor, 16, 19, 46-47
Pele, 14
Pineapple Industry, 16
Places of Interest, 79–89
Plane and Glider Tours, 101
Planetarium, 32
Pohaku O Kauai, 66
Pokai Bay Beach Park, 64,
 95
Polynesian Cultural Center,
 57, 87–88
Portlock, Nathaniel, 14
Pounder's Beach, 57, 93

Index

Princess Kaiulani Hotel, 39
Print House, 23
Punalu'u Beach Park, 58, 93
Punchbowl, 13
Punchbowl Crater, *see* National Memorial Cemetary of the Pacific
Pupukea Beach Park, 53, 92
Pu'u Mai, 45
Pu'u Ohia Trail, 33, 98
Pu'u Ualaka'a State Wayside Park, 33, 82
Pu'uomahuka Heiau, 53
Pu'uomahuka Heiau State Monument, 53–54, 87
Pyle, Ernie, 29

Queen Emma, 23
Queen Emma Summer Palace, 34, 35, 83
Queen Ka'ahumanu, 34
Queen Kamamalu, 22
Queen Liliuokalani, 15, 19, 22, 23,52
Queen Liliuokalani Statue, 79
Queen's Surf Beach, 40

Rabbit Island, *see* Manana Island
Restaurants, 104–112
River Street Pedestrian Mall, 27
Round Top, 33
Royal Bandstand, 22
Royal Coronation Bandstand, 79
Royal Hawaiian Hotel, 16, 36, 38
Royal Hawaiian Shopping Center, 39, 83
Royal House of Oahu, 47
Royal Mausoleum State Monument, 22, 29, 81
Royal Moana Beach, 90

Sacred Falls, 57
Sacred Falls State Park, 57, 88
Sandy Beach Park, 45, 91
Sans Souci State Recreation Area, 42, 90
Schofield Barracks, 16, 49
Scuba Diving, 102
Sea Life Park, 45–46, 85
Seasonal Events, 75
Shark's Cove, 53
Sheraton Moana Surfrider, 39

Sheraton Waikiki, 17, 38
Sightseeing Tours, 101
Snorkeling Excursions, 102
Sportfishing, 103
St. Andrew's Cathedral, 23, 80
St. Peter and Paul Mission, 53
State Capitol, 22, 23, 80
Stevenson, Robert Louis, 42
Sunset Beach Park, 54, 92
Surfing, 103
Swanzy Beach Park, 58, 93

Tahitians, 14
Tantalus, 19, 32–34
Tantalus Mountain, 32
Tennis Courts, 100
Three Tables, 53
Tourist Information, 68
Tours, 100–102
Tropical Lightning Museum, 49, 86
Turtle Bay, 54

U.S. Army Museum, 38
Ulehawa Beach Park #1, 64, 95
Ulehawa Beach Park #2, 64, 95
Ulupo Heiau, 61
Ulupo Heiau State Historical Site, 60–61, 88
US Army Museum, 83
US Bowfin Submarine Museum, 46–47
USS Arizona, 16-17
USS Arizona Memorial, 46, 85
USS Bowfin Submarine Museum and Park, 85

Vacation Rentals, 74
Vancouver, Captain George, 14, 54

Wahiawa, 16, 48
Wahiawa Botanical Gardens, 48, 86
Waiahole, 59
Waialua, 52
Waianae, 64
Waianae Coast, 62–66, *map* 63
Waianae Mountain Range, 13, 18, 47, 62
Waikane, 59
Waikiki, 17, 18, 19, 35–43, *map* 37
Waikiki Aquarium, 41, 84
Waikiki Beach Center, 90

Index

Waikiki Shell, 41
Waimanalo, 55, 61
Waimanalo Bay State
    Recreation Area, 61, 94
Waimanalo Beach Park,
    61, 94, 97
Waimea Bay, 87
Waimea Bay Beach Park,
    52, 92
Waimea Falls, 53
Waimea Falls Park, 53, 87
Waimea Valley, 53
Waipahu, 47–48
Waipahu Garden Cultural
    Park, 48, 86

Wakea, 13
War Memorial, 23
Washington Place, 23, 80
Water Sports, 102–104
Waterskiing, 104
Wheeler Field, 16
Windsurfing, 103
Windward Coast, 55–62, *map* 56
Wo Fat Restaurant, 27
World War II, 16, 29

YWCA, 26